Text Mining with R
A Tidy Approach

Julia Silge and David Robinson

Beijing · Boston · Farnham · Sebastopol · Tokyo

Text Mining with R

by Julia Silge and David Robinson

Published by O'Reilly Media, Inc., 1005 Gravenstein Highway North, Sebastopol, CA 95472.

O'Reilly books may be purchased for educational, business, or sales promotional use. Online editions are also available for most titles (*http://oreilly.com/safari*). For more information, contact our corporate/institutional sales department: 800-998-9938 or *corporate@oreilly.com*.

Editor: Nicole Tache

Production Editor: Nicholas Adams

Copyeditor: Sonia Saruba

Proofreader: Charles Roumeliotis

Indexer: WordCo Indexing Services, Inc.

Interior Designer: David Futato

Cover Designer: Karen Montgomery

Illustrator: Rebecca Demarest

June 2017:   First Edition

Revision History for the First Edition

2017-06-08:   First Release

See *http://oreilly.com/catalog/errata.csp?isbn=9781491981658* for release details.

978-1-491-98165-8

[LSI]

Table of Contents

Preface

If you work in analytics or data science, like we do, you are familiar with the fact that data is being generated all the time at ever faster rates. (You may even be a little weary of people pontificating about this fact.) Analysts are often trained to handle tabular or rectangular data that is mostly numeric, but much of the data proliferating today is unstructured and text-heavy. Many of us who work in analytical fields are not trained in even simple interpretation of natural language.

We developed the tidytext (*https://github.com/juliasilge/tidytext*) (Silge and Robinson 2016) R package because we were familiar with many methods for data wrangling and visualization, but couldn't easily apply these same methods to text. We found that using tidy data principles can make many text mining tasks easier, more effective, and consistent with tools already in wide use. Treating text as data frames of individual words allows us to manipulate, summarize, and visualize the characteristics of text easily, and integrate natural language processing into effective workflows we were already using.

This book serves as an introduction to text mining using the tidytext package and other tidy tools in R. The functions provided by the tidytext package are relatively simple; what is important are the possible applications. Thus, this book provides compelling examples of real text mining problems.

Outline

We start by introducing the tidy text format, and some of the ways dplyr, tidyr, and tidytext allow informative analyses of this structure:

- Chapter 1 outlines the tidy text format and the `unnest_tokens()` function. It also introduces the gutenbergr and janeaustenr packages, which provide useful literary text datasets that we'll use throughout this book.

- Chapter 2 shows how to perform sentiment analysis on a tidy text dataset using the sentiments dataset from tidytext and inner_join() from dplyr.

- Chapter 3 describes the tf-idf statistic (term frequency times inverse document frequency), a quantity used for identifying terms that are especially important to a particular document.

- Chapter 4 introduces n-grams and how to analyze word networks in text using the widyr and ggraph packages.

Text won't be tidy at all stages of an analysis, and it is important to be able to convert back and forth between tidy and nontidy formats:

- Chapter 5 introduces methods for tidying document-term matrices and Corpus objects from the tm and quanteda packages, as well as for casting tidy text datasets into those formats.

- Chapter 6 explores the concept of topic modeling, and uses the tidy() method to interpret and visualize the output of the topicmodels package.

We conclude with several case studies that bring together multiple tidy text mining approaches we've learned:

- Chapter 7 demonstrates an application of a tidy text analysis by analyzing the authors' own Twitter archives. How do Dave's and Julia's tweeting habits compare?

- Chapter 8 explores metadata from over 32,000 NASA datasets (available in JSON) by looking at how keywords from the datasets are connected to title and description fields.

- Chapter 9 analyzes a dataset of Usenet messages from a diverse set of newsgroups (focused on topics like politics, hockey, technology, atheism, and more) to understand patterns across the groups.

Topics This Book Does Not Cover

This book serves as an introduction to the tidy text mining framework, along with a collection of examples, but it is far from a complete exploration of natural language processing. The CRAN Task View on Natural Language Processing (*https://cran.r-project.org/view=NaturalLanguageProcessing*) provides details on other ways to use R for computational linguistics. There are several areas that you may want to explore in more detail according to your needs:

Clustering, classification, and prediction
Machine learning on text is a vast topic that could easily fill its own volume. We introduce one method of unsupervised clustering (topic modeling) in Chapter 6, but many more machine learning algorithms can be used in dealing with text.

Word embedding
One popular modern approach for text analysis is to map words to vector representations, which can then be used to examine linguistic relationships between words and to classify text. Such representations of words are not tidy in the sense that we consider here, but have found powerful applications in machine learning algorithms.

More complex tokenization
The tidytext package trusts the tokenizers package (Mullen 2016) to perform tokenization, which itself wraps a variety of tokenizers with a consistent interface, but many others exist for specific applications.

Languages other than English
Some of our users have had success applying tidytext to their text mining needs for languages other than English, but we don't cover any such examples in this book.

About This Book

This book is focused on practical software examples and data explorations. There are few equations, but a great deal of code. We especially focus on generating real insights from the literature, news, and social media that we analyze.

We don't assume any previous knowledge of text mining. Professional linguists and text analysts will likely find our examples elementary, though we are confident they can build on the framework for their own analyses.

We assume that the reader is at least slightly familiar with dplyr, ggplot2, and the %>% "pipe" operator in R, and is interested in applying these tools to text data. For users who don't have this background, we recommend books such as *R for Data Science* (*http://r4ds.had.co.nz/*) by Hadley Wickham and Garrett Grolemund (O'Reilly). We believe that with a basic background and interest in tidy data, even a user early in his or her R career can understand and apply our examples.

 If you are reading a printed copy of this book, the images have been rendered in grayscale rather than color. To view the color versions, see the book's GitHub page (*https://github.com/dgrtwo/tidy-text-mining*).

Conventions Used in This Book

The following typographical conventions are used in this book:

Italic

Indicates new terms, URLs, email addresses, filenames, and file extensions.

`Constant width`

Used for program listings, as well as within paragraphs to refer to program elements such as variable or function names, databases, data types, environment variables, statements, and keywords.

`Constant width bold`

Shows commands or other text that should be typed literally by the user.

`Constant width italic`

Shows text that should be replaced with user-supplied values or by values determined by context.

This element signifies a tip or suggestion.

This element signifies a general note.

This element indicates a warning or caution.

Using Code Examples

While we show the code behind the vast majority of the analyses, in the interest of space we sometimes choose not to show the code generating a particular visualization if we've already provided the code for several similar graphs. We trust the reader can learn from and build on our examples, and the code used to generate the book can be found in our public GitHub repository (*https://github.com/dgrtwo/tidy-text-mining*).

This book is here to help you get your job done. In general, if example code is offered with this book, you may use it in your programs and documentation. You do not need to contact us for permission unless you're reproducing a significant portion of the code. For example, writing a program that uses several chunks of code from this book does not require permission. Selling or distributing a CD-ROM of examples from O'Reilly books does require permission. Answering a question by citing this book and quoting example code does not require permission. Incorporating a significant amount of example code from this book into your product's documentation does require permission.

We appreciate, but do not require, attribution. An attribution usually includes the title, author, publisher, and ISBN. For example: "*Text Mining with R* by Julia Silge and David Robinson (O'Reilly). Copyright 2017 Julia Silge and David Robinson, 978-1-491-98165-8."

If you feel your use of code examples falls outside fair use or the permission given above, feel free to contact us at *permissions@oreilly.com*.

O'Reilly Safari

 *Safari* (formerly Safari Books Online) is a membership-based training and reference platform for enterprise, government, educators, and individuals.

Members have access to thousands of books, training videos, Learning Paths, interactive tutorials, and curated playlists from over 250 publishers, including O'Reilly Media, Harvard Business Review, Prentice Hall Professional, Addison-Wesley Professional, Microsoft Press, Sams, Que, Peachpit Press, Adobe, Focal Press, Cisco Press, John Wiley & Sons, Syngress, Morgan Kaufmann, IBM Redbooks, Packt, Adobe Press, FT Press, Apress, Manning, New Riders, McGraw-Hill, Jones & Bartlett, and Course Technology, among others.

For more information, please visit *http://oreilly.com/safari*.

How to Contact Us

Please address comments and questions concerning this book to the publisher:

O'Reilly Media, Inc.
1005 Gravenstein Highway North
Sebastopol, CA 95472
800-998-9938 (in the United States or Canada)
707-829-0515 (international or local)
707-829-0104 (fax)

To comment or ask technical questions about this book, send email to *bookquestions@oreilly.com*.

For more information about our books, courses, conferences, and news, see our website at *http://www.oreilly.com*.

Find us on Facebook: *http://facebook.com/oreilly*

Follow us on Twitter: *http://twitter.com/oreillymedia*

Watch us on YouTube: *http://www.youtube.com/oreillymedia*

Acknowledgements

We are so thankful for the contributions, help, and perspectives of people who have moved us forward in this project. There are several people and organizations we would like to thank in particular.

We would like to thank Oliver Keyes and Gabriela de Queiroz for their contributions to the tidytext package, Lincoln Mullen for his work on the tokenizers (*https://github.com/ropensci/tokenizers*) package, Kenneth Benoit for his work on the quanteda (*https://github.com/kbenoit/quanteda*) package, Thomas Pedersen for his work on the ggraph (*https://github.com/thomasp85/ggraph*) package, and Hadley Wickham for his work in framing tidy data principles and building tidy tools. We would also like to thank Karthik Ram and rOpenSci (*https://ropensci.org/*), who hosted us at the unconference where we began work, and the NASA Datanauts (*https://open.nasa.gov/explore/datanauts/*) program, for the opportunities and support they have provided Julia during her time with them.

We received thoughtful, thorough technical reviews that improved the quality of this book significantly. We would like to thank Mara Averick, Carolyn Clayton, Simon Jackson, Sean Kross, and Lincoln Mullen for their investment of time and energy in these technical reviews.

This book was written in the open, and several people contributed via pull requests or issues. Special thanks goes to those who contributed via GitHub: @ainilaha, Brian G. Barkley, Jon Calder, @eijoac, Marc Ferradou, Jonathan Gilligan, Matthew Henderson, Simon Jackson, @jedgore, @kanishkamisra, Josiah Parry, @suyi19890508, Stephen Turner, and Yihui Xie.

Finally, we want to dedicate this book to our spouses, Robert and Dana. We both could produce a great deal of sentimental text on this subject but will restrict ourselves to heartfelt thanks.

## CHAPTER 1

The Tidy Text Format

Using tidy data principles is a powerful way to make handling data easier and more effective, and this is no less true when it comes to dealing with text. As described by Hadley Wickham (Wickham 2014), tidy data has a specific structure:

- Each variable is a column.
- Each observation is a row.
- Each type of observational unit is a table.

We thus define the tidy text format as being *a table with one token per row*. A token is a meaningful unit of text, such as a word, that we are interested in using for analysis, and tokenization is the process of splitting text into tokens. This one-token-per-row structure is in contrast to the ways text is often stored in current analyses, perhaps as strings or in a document-term matrix. For tidy text mining, the *token* that is stored in each row is most often a single word, but can also be an n-gram, sentence, or paragraph. In the tidytext package, we provide functionality to tokenize by commonly used units of text like these and convert to a one-term-per-row format.

Tidy data sets allow manipulation with a standard set of "tidy" tools, including popular packages such as dplyr (Wickham and Francois 2016), tidyr (Wickham 2016), ggplot2 (Wickham 2009), and broom (Robinson 2017). By keeping the input and output in tidy tables, users can transition fluidly between these packages. We've found these tidy tools extend naturally to many text analyses and explorations.

At the same time, the tidytext package doesn't expect a user to keep text data in a tidy form at all times during an analysis. The package includes functions to `tidy()` objects (see the broom package [Robinson, cited above]) from popular text mining R packages such as tm (Feinerer et al. 2008) and quanteda (Benoit and Nulty 2016). This allows, for example, a workflow where importing, filtering, and processing is done using dplyr and other tidy tools, after which the data is converted into a document-term matrix for machine learning applications. The models can then be reconverted into a tidy form for interpretation and visualization with ggplot2.

Contrasting Tidy Text with Other Data Structures

As we stated above, we define the tidy text format as being a table with *one token per row*. Structuring text data in this way means that it conforms to tidy data principles and can be manipulated with a set of consistent tools. This is worth contrasting with the ways text is often stored in text mining approaches:

String
> Text can, of course, be stored as strings (i.e., character vectors) within R, and often text data is first read into memory in this form.

Corpus
> These types of objects typically contain raw strings annotated with additional metadata and details.

Document-term matrix
> This is a sparse matrix describing a collection (i.e., a corpus) of documents with one row for each document and one column for each term. The value in the matrix is typically word count or tf-idf (see Chapter 3).

Let's hold off on exploring corpus and document-term matrix objects until Chapter 5, and get down to the basics of converting text to a tidy format.

The unnest_tokens Function

Emily Dickinson wrote some lovely text in her time.

```
text <- c("Because I could not stop for Death -",
          "He kindly stopped for me -",
          "The Carriage held but just Ourselves -",
          "and Immortality")

text

## [1] "Because I could not stop for Death -"   "He kindly stopped for me -"
## [3] "The Carriage held but just Ourselves -" "and Immortality"
```

This is a typical character vector that we might want to analyze. In order to turn it into a tidy text dataset, we first need to put it into a data frame.

```
library(dplyr)
text_df <- data_frame(line = 1:4, text = text)

text_df
```

```
## # A tibble: 4 × 2
##    line                                    text
##   <int>                                   <chr>
## 1    1    Because I could not stop for Death -
## 2    2              He kindly stopped for me -
## 3    3 The Carriage held but just Ourselves -
## 4    4                        and Immortality
```

What does it mean that this data frame has printed out as a "tibble"? A *tibble* is a modern class of data frame within R, available in the dplyr and tibble packages, that has a convenient print method, will not convert strings to factors, and does not use row names. Tibbles are great for use with tidy tools.

Notice that this data frame containing text isn't yet compatible with tidy text analysis. We can't filter out words or count which occur most frequently, since each row is made up of multiple combined words. We need to convert this so that it has *one token per document per row*.

 A token is a meaningful unit of text, most often a word, that we are interested in using for further analysis, and tokenization is the process of splitting text into tokens.

In this first example, we only have one document (the poem), but we will explore examples with multiple documents soon.

Within our tidy text framework, we need to both break the text into individual tokens (a process called *tokenization*) *and* transform it to a tidy data structure. To do this, we use the tidytext `unnest_tokens()` function.

```
library(tidytext)

text_df %>%
  unnest_tokens(word, text)
```

```
## # A tibble: 20 × 2
##     line    word
##    <int>   <chr>
## 1      1 because
## 2      1       i
## 3      1   could
## 4      1     not
## 5      1    stop
## 6      1     for
## 7      1   death
## 8      2      he
## 9      2  kindly
## 10     2 stopped
## # ... with 10 more rows
```

The two basic arguments to `unnest_tokens` used here are column names. First we have the output column name that will be created as the text is unnested into it (`word`, in this case), and then the input column that the text comes from (`text`, in this case). Remember that `text_df` above has a column called `text` that contains the data of interest.

After using `unnest_tokens`, we've split each row so that there is one token (word) in each row of the new data frame; the default tokenization in `unnest_tokens()` is for single words, as shown here. Also notice:

- Other columns, such as the line number each word came from, are retained.
- Punctuation has been stripped.
- By default, `unnest_tokens()` converts the tokens to lowercase, which makes them easier to compare or combine with other datasets. (Use the `to_lower = FALSE` argument to turn off this behavior).

Having the text data in this format lets us manipulate, process, and visualize the text using the standard set of tidy tools, namely dplyr, tidyr, and ggplot2, as shown in Figure 1-1.

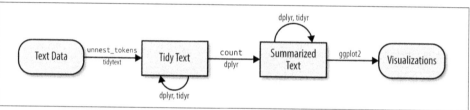

Figure 1-1. A flowchart of a typical text analysis using tidy data principles. This chapter shows how to summarize and visualize text using these tools.

Tidying the Works of Jane Austen

Let's use the text of Jane Austen's six completed, published novels from the janeaustenr (*https://cran.r-project.org/package=janeaustenr*) package (Silge 2016), and transform them into a tidy format. The janeaustenr package provides these texts in a one-row-per-line format, where a line in this context is analogous to a literal printed line in a physical book. Let's start with that, and also use `mutate()` to annotate a `linenum` ber quantity to keep track of lines in the original format, and a `chapter` (using a regex) to find where all the chapters are.

```
library(janeaustenr)
library(dplyr)
library(stringr)

original_books <- austen_books() %>%
```

```
    group_by(book) %>%
    mutate(linenumber = row_number(),
            chapter = cumsum(str_detect(text, regex("^chapter [\\divxlc]",
                                                     ignore_case = TRUE)))) %>%
    ungroup()

original_books

## # A tibble: 73,422 × 4
##                         text            book linenumber chapter
##                         <chr>           <fctr>   <int>   <int>
## 1  SENSE AND SENSIBILITY Sense & Sensibility      1       0
## 2                         Sense & Sensibility      2       0
## 3        by Jane Austen Sense & Sensibility      3       0
## 4                         Sense & Sensibility      4       0
## 5                (1811) Sense & Sensibility      5       0
## 6                         Sense & Sensibility      6       0
## 7                         Sense & Sensibility      7       0
## 8                         Sense & Sensibility      8       0
## 9                         Sense & Sensibility      9       0
## 10            CHAPTER 1 Sense & Sensibility     10       1
## # ... with 73,412 more rows
```

To work with this as a tidy dataset, we need to restructure it in the *one-token-per-row* format, which as we saw earlier is done with the unnest_tokens() function.

```
library(tidytext)
tidy_books <- original_books %>%
  unnest_tokens(word, text)

tidy_books

## # A tibble: 725,054 × 4
##                    book linenumber chapter        word
##                    <fctr>    <int>   <int>       <chr>
## 1  Sense & Sensibility       1       0       sense
## 2  Sense & Sensibility       1       0         and
## 3  Sense & Sensibility       1       0 sensibility
## 4  Sense & Sensibility       3       0          by
## 5  Sense & Sensibility       3       0        jane
## 6  Sense & Sensibility       3       0      austen
## 7  Sense & Sensibility       5       0        1811
## 8  Sense & Sensibility      10       1     chapter
## 9  Sense & Sensibility      10       1           1
## 10 Sense & Sensibility      13       1         the
## # ... with 725,044 more rows
```

This function uses the tokenizers (*https://github.com/ropensci/tokenizers*) package to separate each line of text in the original data frame into tokens. The default tokenizing is for words, but other options include characters, n-grams, sentences, lines, paragraphs, or separation around a regex pattern.

Now that the data is in one-word-per-row format, we can manipulate it with tidy tools like dplyr. Often in text analysis, we will want to remove *stop words*, which are words that are not useful for an analysis, typically extremely common words such as "the," "of," "to," and so forth in English. We can remove stop words (kept in the tidy-text dataset stop_words) with an anti_join().

```
data(stop_words)

tidy_books <- tidy_books %>%
  anti_join(stop_words)
```

The stop_words dataset in the tidytext package contains stop words from three lexicons. We can use them all together, as we have here, or filter() to only use one set of stop words if that is more appropriate for a certain analysis.

We can also use dplyr's count() to find the most common words in all the books as a whole.

```
tidy_books %>%
  count(word, sort = TRUE)

## # A tibble: 13,914 × 2
##       word      n
##      <chr> <int>
## 1     miss  1855
## 2     time  1337
## 3    fanny   862
## 4     dear   822
## 5     lady   817
## 6      sir   806
## 7      day   797
## 8     emma   787
## 9   sister   727
## 10   house   699
## # ... with 13,904 more rows
```

Because we've been using tidy tools, our word counts are stored in a tidy data frame. This allows us to pipe directly to the ggplot2 package, for example to create a visualization of the most common words (Figure 1-2).

```
library(ggplot2)

tidy_books %>%
  count(word, sort = TRUE) %>%
  filter(n > 600) %>%
  mutate(word = reorder(word, n)) %>%
  ggplot(aes(word, n)) +
  geom_col() +
  xlab(NULL) +
  coord_flip()
```

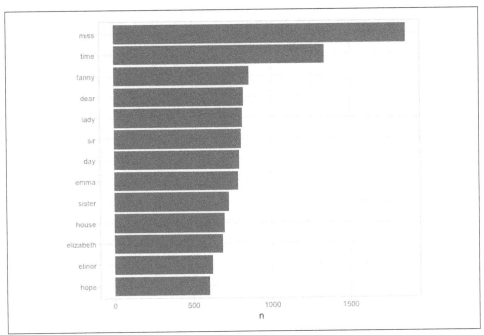

Figure 1-2. The most common words in Jane Austen's novels

Note that the `austen_books()` function started us with exactly the text we wanted to analyze, but in other cases we may need to perform cleaning of text data, such as removing copyright headers or formatting. You'll see examples of this kind of pre-processing in the case study chapters, particularly "Preprocessing" on page 153.

The gutenbergr Package

Now that we've used the janeaustenr package to explore tidying text, let's introduce the gutenbergr (*https://github.com/ropenscilabs/gutenbergr*) package (Robinson 2016). The gutenbergr package provides access to the public domain works from the Project Gutenberg (*https://www.gutenberg.org/*) collection. The package includes tools both for downloading books (stripping out the unhelpful header/footer information), and a complete dataset of Project Gutenberg metadata that can be used to find works of interest. In this book, we will mostly use the `gutenberg_download()` function that downloads one or more works from Project Gutenberg by ID, but you can also use other functions to explore metadata, pair Gutenberg ID with title, author, language, and so on, or gather information about authors.

To learn more about gutenbergr, check out the package's tutorial at rOpenSci *(https://ropensci.org/tutorials/gutenbergr_tutorial.html)*, where it is one of rOpenSci's packages for data access.

Word Frequencies

A common task in text mining is to look at word frequencies, just like we have done above for Jane Austen's novels, and to compare frequencies across different texts. We can do this intuitively and smoothly using tidy data principles. We already have Jane Austen's works; let's get two more sets of texts to compare to. First, let's look at some science fiction and fantasy novels by H.G. Wells, who lived in the late 19th and early 20th centuries. Let's get *The Time Machine (https://www.gutenberg.org/ebooks/35)*, *The War of the Worlds (https://www.gutenberg.org/ebooks/36)*, *The Invisible Man (https://www.gutenberg.org/ebooks/5230)*, and *The Island of Doctor Moreau (https://www.gutenberg.org/ebooks/159)*. We can access these works using `gutenberg_download()` and the Project Gutenberg ID numbers for each novel.

```
library(gutenbergr)

hgwells <- gutenberg_download(c(35, 36, 5230, 159))

tidy_hgwells <- hgwells %>%
  unnest_tokens(word, text) %>%
  anti_join(stop_words)
```

Just for kicks, what are the most common words in these novels of H.G. Wells?

```
tidy_hgwells %>%
  count(word, sort = TRUE)
## # A tibble: 11,769 × 2
##       word     n
##      <chr> <int>
## 1     time   454
## 2   people   302
## 3     door   260
## 4    heard   249
## 5    black   232
## 6    stood   229
## 7    white   222
## 8     hand   218
## 9     kemp   213
## 10    eyes   210
## # ... with 11,759 more rows
```

Now let's get some well-known works of the Brontë sisters, whose lives overlapped with Jane Austen's somewhat, but who wrote in a rather different style. Let's get *Jane Eyre (https://www.gutenberg.org/ebooks/1260)*, *Wuthering Heights (https://www.guten*

berg.org/ebooks/768), *The Tenant of Wildfell Hall* (*https://www.gutenberg.org/ebooks/969*), *Villette* (*https://www.gutenberg.org/ebooks/9182*), and *Agnes Grey* (*https://www.gutenberg.org/ebooks/767*). We will again use the Project Gutenberg ID numbers for each novel and access the texts using `gutenberg_download()`.

```
bronte <- gutenberg_download(c(1260, 768, 969, 9182, 767))

tidy_bronte <- bronte %>%
  unnest_tokens(word, text) %>%
  anti_join(stop_words)
```

What are the most common words in these novels of the Brontë sisters?

```
tidy_bronte %>%
  count(word, sort = TRUE)

## # A tibble: 23,051 × 2
##       word     n
##      <chr> <int>
## 1     time  1065
## 2     miss   855
## 3      day   827
## 4     hand   768
## 5     eyes   713
## 6    night   647
## 7    heart   638
## 8   looked   602
## 9     door   592
## 10    half   586
## # ... with 23,041 more rows
```

Interesting that "time," "eyes," and "hand" are in the top 10 for both H.G. Wells and the Brontë sisters.

Now, let's calculate the frequency for each word in the works of Jane Austen, the Brontë sisters, and H.G. Wells by binding the data frames together. We can use `spread` and `gather` from tidyr to reshape our data frame so that it is just what we need for plotting and comparing the three sets of novels.

```
library(tidyr)

frequency <- bind_rows(mutate(tidy_bronte, author = "Brontë Sisters"),
                       mutate(tidy_hgwells, author = "H.G. Wells"),
                       mutate(tidy_books, author = "Jane Austen")) %>%
  mutate(word = str_extract(word, "[a-z']+")) %>%
  count(author, word) %>%
  group_by(author) %>%
  mutate(proportion = n / sum(n)) %>%
  select(-n) %>%
  spread(author, proportion) %>%
  gather(author, proportion, `Brontë Sisters`:`H.G. Wells`)
```

We use str_extract() here because the UTF-8 encoded texts from Project Gutenberg have some examples of words with underscores around them to indicate emphasis (like italics). The tokenizer treated these as words, but we don't want to count *"any"* separately from "any" as we saw in our initial data exploration before choosing to use str_extract().

Now let's plot (Figure 1-3).

```
library(scales)

# expect a warning about rows with missing values being removed
ggplot(frequency, aes(x = proportion, y = `Jane Austen`,
                      color = abs(`Jane Austen` - proportion))) +
  geom_abline(color = "gray40", lty = 2) +
  geom_jitter(alpha = 0.1, size = 2.5, width = 0.3, height = 0.3) +
  geom_text(aes(label = word), check_overlap = TRUE, vjust = 1.5) +
  scale_x_log10(labels = percent_format()) +
  scale_y_log10(labels = percent_format()) +
  scale_color_gradient(limits = c(0, 0.001),
                       low = "darkslategray4", high = "gray75") +
  facet_wrap(~author, ncol = 2) +
  theme(legend.position="none") +
  labs(y = "Jane Austen", x = NULL)
```

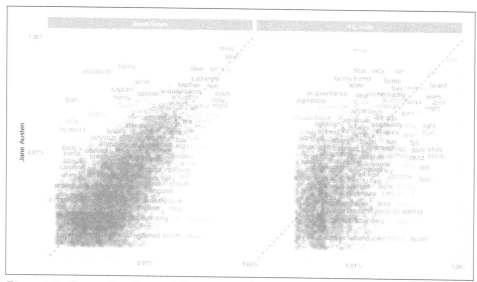

Figure 1-3. Comparing the word frequencies of Jane Austen, the Brontë sisters, and H.G. Wells

Words that are close to the line in these plots have similar frequencies in both sets of texts, for example, in both Austen and Brontë texts ("miss," "time," and "day" at the high frequency end) or in both Austen and Wells texts ("time," "day," and "brother" at the high frequency end). Words that are far from the line are words that are found more in one set of texts than another. For example, in the Austen-Brontë panel, words like "elizabeth," "emma," and "fanny" (all proper nouns) are found in Austen's texts but not much in the Brontë texts, while words like "arthur" and "dog" are found in the Brontë texts but not the Austen texts. In comparing H.G. Wells with Jane Austen, Wells uses words like "beast," "guns," "feet," and "black" that Austen does not, while Austen uses words like "family", "friend," "letter," and "dear" that Wells does not.

Overall, notice in Figure 1-3 that the words in the Austen-Brontë panel are closer to the zero-slope line than in the Austen-Wells panel. Also notice that the words extend to lower frequencies in the Austen-Brontë panel; there is empty space in the Austen-Wells panel at low frequency. These characteristics indicate that Austen and the Brontë sisters use more similar words than Austen and H.G. Wells. Also, we see that not all the words are found in all three sets of texts, and there are fewer data points in the panel for Austen and H.G. Wells.

Let's quantify how similar and different these sets of word frequencies are using a correlation test. How correlated are the word frequencies between Austen and the Brontë sisters, and between Austen and Wells?

```
cor.test(data = frequency[frequency$author == "Brontë Sisters",],
         ~ proportion + `Jane Austen`)

##
##  Pearson's product-moment correlation
##
## data:  proportion and Jane Austen
## t = 119.64, df = 10404, p-value < 2.2e-16
## alternative hypothesis: true correlation is not equal to 0
## 95 percent confidence interval:
##  0.7527837 0.7689611
## sample estimates:
##       cor
## 0.7609907

cor.test(data = frequency[frequency$author == "H.G. Wells",],
         ~ proportion + `Jane Austen`)

##
##  Pearson's product-moment correlation
##
## data:  proportion and Jane Austen
## t = 36.441, df = 6053, p-value < 2.2e-16
## alternative hypothesis: true correlation is not equal to 0
## 95 percent confidence interval:
##  0.4032820 0.4446006
## sample estimates:
##       cor
## 0.424162
```

Just as we saw in the plots, the word frequencies are more correlated between the Austen and Brontë novels than between Austen and H.G. Wells.

Summary

In this chapter, we explored what we mean by tidy data when it comes to text, and how tidy data principles can be applied to natural language processing. When text is organized in a format with one token per row, tasks like removing stop words or calculating word frequencies are natural applications of familiar operations within the tidy tool ecosystem. The one-token-per-row framework can be extended from single words to n-grams and other meaningful units of text, as well as to many other analysis priorities that we will consider in this book.

## CHAPTER 2

Sentiment Analysis with Tidy Data

In the previous chapter, we explored in depth what we mean by the tidy text format and showed how this format can be used to approach questions about word frequency. This allowed us to analyze which words are used most frequently in documents and to compare documents, but now let's investigate a different topic. Let's address the topic of opinion mining or sentiment analysis. When human readers approach a text, we use our understanding of the emotional intent of words to infer whether a section of text is positive or negative, or perhaps characterized by some other more nuanced emotion like surprise or disgust. We can use the tools of text mining to approach the emotional content of text programmatically, as shown in Figure 2-1.

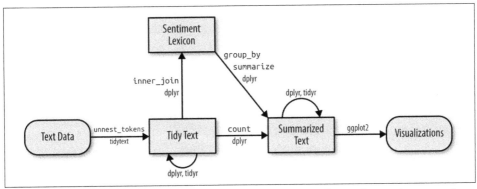

Figure 2-1. A flowchart of a typical text analysis that uses tidytext for sentiment analysis. This chapter shows how to implement sentiment analysis using tidy data principles.

One way to analyze the sentiment of a text is to consider the text as a combination of its individual words, and the sentiment content of the whole text as the sum of the sentiment content of the individual words. This isn't the only way to approach sentiment analysis, but it is an often-used approach, *and* an approach that naturally takes advantage of the tidy tool ecosystem.

The sentiments Dataset

As discussed above, there are a variety of methods and dictionaries that exist for evaluating opinion or emotion in text. The tidytext package contains several sentiment lexicons in the `sentiments` dataset.

```
library(tidytext)

sentiments

## # A tibble: 27,314 × 4
##            word sentiment lexicon score
##           <chr>     <chr>   <chr> <int>
## 1        abacus     trust     nrc    NA
## 2       abandon      fear     nrc    NA
## 3       abandon  negative     nrc    NA
## 4       abandon   sadness     nrc    NA
## 5     abandoned     anger     nrc    NA
## 6     abandoned      fear     nrc    NA
## 7     abandoned  negative     nrc    NA
## 8     abandoned   sadness     nrc    NA
## 9   abandonment     anger     nrc    NA
## 10  abandonment      fear     nrc    NA
## # ... with 27,304 more rows
```

The three general-purpose lexicons are:

- AFINN from Finn Årup Nielsen (*http://bit.ly/2s50F5w*)
- Bing from Bing Liu and collaborators (*http://bit.ly/2s4B254*)
- NRC from Saif Mohammad and Peter Turney (*http://bit.ly/2s4B8ts*)

All three lexicons are based on unigrams, i.e., single words. These lexicons contain many English words and the words are assigned scores for positive/negative sentiment, and also possibly emotions like joy, anger, sadness, and so forth. The NRC lexicon categorizes words in a binary fashion ("yes"/"no") into categories of positive, negative, anger, anticipation, disgust, fear, joy, sadness, surprise, and trust. The Bing lexicon categorizes words in a binary fashion into positive and negative categories. The AFINN lexicon assigns words with a score that runs between -5 and 5, with negative scores indicating negative sentiment and positive scores indicating positive sentiment. All of this information is tabulated in the `sentiments` dataset, and tidytext provides the function `get_sentiments()` to get specific sentiment lexicons without the columns that are not used in that lexicon.

```
get_sentiments("afinn")

## # A tibble: 2,476 × 2
##             word score
##            <chr> <int>
## 1        abandon    -2
## 2      abandoned    -2
## 3       abandons    -2
## 4       abducted    -2
## 5      abduction    -2
## 6     abductions    -2
## 7          abhor    -3
## 8       abhorred    -3
## 9      abhorrent    -3
## 10        abhors    -3
## # ... with 2,466 more rows

get_sentiments("bing")

## # A tibble: 6,788 × 2
##             word sentiment
##            <chr>     <chr>
## 1        2-faced  negative
## 2        2-faces  negative
## 3             a+  positive
## 4       abnormal  negative
## 5        abolish  negative
## 6     abominable  negative
## 7     abominably  negative
## 8      abominate  negative
## 9     abomination negative
## 10         abort  negative
## # ... with 6,778 more rows

get_sentiments("nrc")

## # A tibble: 13,901 × 2
##             word sentiment
##            <chr>     <chr>
## 1         abacus     trust
## 2        abandon      fear
## 3        abandon  negative
## 4        abandon   sadness
## 5      abandoned     anger
## 6      abandoned      fear
## 7      abandoned  negative
## 8      abandoned   sadness
## 9    abandonment     anger
## 10   abandonment      fear
## # ... with 13,891 more rows
```

How were these sentiment lexicons put together and validated? They were constructed via either crowdsourcing (using, for example, Amazon Mechanical Turk) or by the labor of one of the authors, and were validated using some combination of crowdsourcing again, restaurant or movie reviews, or Twitter data. Given this information, we may hesitate to apply these sentiment lexicons to styles of text dramatically different from what they were validated on, such as narrative fiction from 200 years ago. While it is true that using these sentiment lexicons with, for example, Jane Austen's novels may give us less accurate results than with tweets sent by a contemporary writer, we still can measure the sentiment content for words that are shared across the lexicon and the text.

There are also some domain-specific sentiment lexicons available, constructed to be used with text from a specific content area. "Example: Mining Financial Articles" on page 81 explores an analysis using a sentiment lexicon specifically for finance.

 Dictionary-based methods like the ones we are discussing find the total sentiment of a piece of text by adding up the individual sentiment scores for each word in the text.

Not every English word is in the lexicons because many English words are pretty neutral. It is important to keep in mind that these methods do not take into account qualifiers before a word, such as in "no good" or "not true"; a lexicon-based method like this is based on unigrams only. For many kinds of text (like the narrative examples below), there are no sustained sections of sarcasm or negated text, so this is not an important effect. Also, we can use a tidy text approach to begin to understand what kinds of negation words are important in a given text; see Chapter 9 for an extended example of such an analysis.

One last caveat is that the size of the chunk of text that we use to add up unigram sentiment scores can have an effect on an analysis. A text the size of many paragraphs can often have positive and negative sentiment averaging out to about zero, while sentence-sized or paragraph-sized text often works better.

Sentiment Analysis with Inner Join

With data in a tidy format, sentiment analysis can be done as an inner join. This is another of the great successes of viewing text mining as a tidy data analysis task— much as removing stop words is an anti-join operation, performing sentiment analysis is an inner join operation.

Let's look at the words with a joy score from the NRC lexicon. What are the most common joy words in *Emma*? First, we need to take the text of the novel and convert the text to the tidy format using unnest_tokens(), just as we did in "Tidying the Works of Jane Austen" on page 4. Let's also set up some other columns to keep track of which line and chapter of the book each word comes from; we use `group_by` and `mutate` to construct those columns.

```
library(janeaustenr)
library(dplyr)
library(stringr)

tidy_books <- austen_books() %>%
  group_by(book) %>%
  mutate(linenumber = row_number(),
         chapter = cumsum(str_detect(text, regex("^chapter [\\divxlc]",
                                                 ignore_case = TRUE)))) %>%
  ungroup() %>%
  unnest_tokens(word, text)
```

Notice that we chose the name `word` for the output column from `unnest_tokens()`. This is a convenient choice because the sentiment lexicons and stop-word datasets have columns named `word`; performing inner joins and anti-joins is thus easier.

Now that the text is in a tidy format with one word per row, we are ready to do the sentiment analysis. First, let's use the NRC lexicon and `filter()` for the joy words. Next, let's `filter()` the data frame with the text from the book for the words from *Emma* and then use `inner_join()` to perform the sentiment analysis. What are the most common joy words in *Emma*? Let's use `count()` from dplyr.

```
nrcjoy <- get_sentiments("nrc") %>%
  filter(sentiment == "joy")

tidy_books %>%
  filter(book == "Emma") %>%
  inner_join(nrcjoy) %>%
  count(word, sort = TRUE)

## # A tibble: 303 × 2
##        word     n
##       <chr> <int>
## 1      good   359
## 2     young   192
## 3    friend   166
## 4      hope   143
## 5     happy   125
## 6      love   117
## 7      deal    92
## 8     found    92
## 9   present    89
## 10     kind    82
## # ... with 293 more rows
```

We see many positive, happy words about hope, friendship, and love here.

Or instead we could examine how sentiment changes throughout each novel. We can do this with just a handful of lines that are mostly dplyr functions. First, we find a sentiment score for each word using the Bing lexicon and `inner_join()`.

Next, we count up how many positive and negative words there are in defined sections of each book. We define an `index` here to keep track of where we are in the narrative; this index (using integer division) counts up sections of 80 lines of text.

 The `%/%` operator does integer division (x `%/%` y is equivalent to `floor(x/y)`) so the index keeps track of which 80-line section of text we are counting up negative and positive sentiment in.

Small sections of text may not have enough words in them to get a good estimate of sentiment, while really large sections can wash out narrative structure. For these books, using 80 lines works well, but this can vary depending on individual texts, how long the lines were to start with, etc. We then use `spread()` so that we have negative and positive sentiment in separate columns, and lastly calculate a net sentiment (`positive - negative`).

```
library(tidyr)

janeaustensentiment <- tidy_books %>%
  inner_join(get_sentiments("bing")) %>%
  count(book, index = linenumber %/% 80, sentiment) %>%
  spread(sentiment, n, fill = 0) %>%
  mutate(sentiment = positive - negative)
```

Now we can plot these sentiment scores across the plot trajectory of each novel. Notice that we are plotting against the `index` on the x-axis that keeps track of narrative time in sections of text (Figure 2-2).

```
library(ggplot2)

ggplot(janeaustensentiment, aes(index, sentiment, fill = book)) +
  geom_col(show.legend = FALSE) +
  facet_wrap(~book, ncol = 2, scales = "free_x")
```

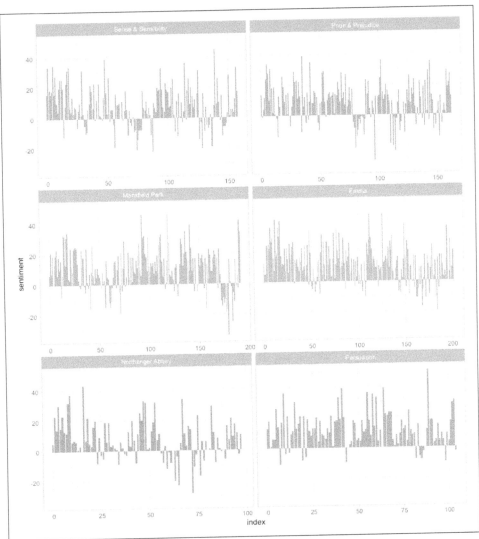

Figure 2-2. Sentiment through the narratives of Jane Austen's novels

We can see in Figure 2-2 how the plot of each novel changes toward more positive or negative sentiment over the trajectory of the story.

Comparing the Three Sentiment Dictionaries

With several options for sentiment lexicons, you might want some more information on which one is appropriate for your purposes. Let's use all three sentiment lexicons and examine how the sentiment changes across the narrative arc of *Pride and Preju-*

dice. First, let's use `filter()` to choose only the words from the one novel we are interested in.

```
pride_prejudice <- tidy_books %>%
  filter(book == "Pride & Prejudice")

pride_prejudice

## # A tibble: 122,204 × 4
##                  book linenumber chapter      word
##                <fctr>      <int>   <int>     <chr>
## 1  Pride & Prejudice           1       0     pride
## 2  Pride & Prejudice           1       0       and
## 3  Pride & Prejudice           1       0 prejudice
## 4  Pride & Prejudice           3       0        by
## 5  Pride & Prejudice           3       0      jane
## 6  Pride & Prejudice           3       0    austen
## 7  Pride & Prejudice           7       1   chapter
## 8  Pride & Prejudice           7       1         1
## 9  Pride & Prejudice          10       1        it
## 10 Pride & Prejudice          10       1        is
## # ... with 122,194 more rows
```

Now, we can use `inner_join()` to calculate the sentiment in different ways.

 Remember from above that the AFINN lexicon measures sentiment with a numeric score between -5 and 5, while the other two lexicons categorize words in a binary fashion, either positive or negative. To find a sentiment score in chunks of text throughout the novel, we will need to use a different pattern for the AFINN lexicon than for the other two.

Let's again use integer division (%/%) to define larger sections of text that span multiple lines, and we can use the same pattern with `count()`, `spread()`, and `mutate()` to find the net sentiment in each of these sections of text.

```
afinn <- pride_prejudice %>%
  inner_join(get_sentiments("afinn")) %>%
  group_by(index = linenumber %/% 80) %>%
  summarise(sentiment = sum(score)) %>%
  mutate(method = "AFINN")

bing_and_nrc <- bind_rows(
  pride_prejudice %>%
    inner_join(get_sentiments("bing")) %>%
    mutate(method = "Bing et al."),
  pride_prejudice %>%
    inner_join(get_sentiments("nrc") %>%
                  filter(sentiment %in% c("positive",
                                          "negative"))) %>%
    mutate(method = "NRC")) %>%
```

```
count(method, index = linenumber %/% 80, sentiment) %>%
spread(sentiment, n, fill = 0) %>%
mutate(sentiment = positive - negative)
```

We now have an estimate of the net sentiment (`positive - negative`) in each chunk of the novel text for each sentiment lexicon. Let's bind them together and visualize them in Figure 2-3.

```
bind_rows(afinn,
          bing_and_nrc) %>%
  ggplot(aes(index, sentiment, fill = method)) +
  geom_col(show.legend = FALSE) +
  facet_wrap(~method, ncol = 1, scales = "free_y")
```

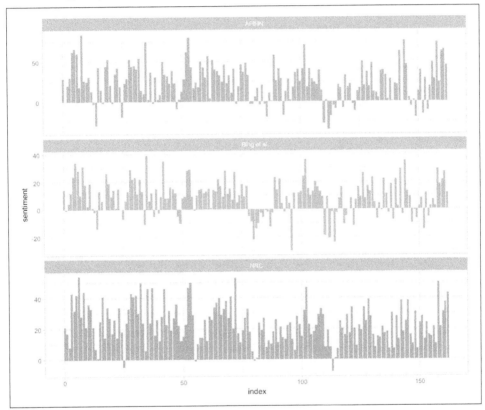

Figure 2-3. Comparing three sentiment lexicons using Pride and Prejudice

The three different lexicons for calculating sentiment give results that are different in an absolute sense but have similar relative trajectories through the novel. We see similar dips and peaks in sentiment at about the same places in the novel, but the absolute values are significantly different. The AFINN lexicon gives the largest absolute values, with high positive values. The lexicon from Bing et al. has lower absolute values and seems to label larger blocks of contiguous positive or negative text. The NRC results are shifted higher relative to the other two, labeling the text more positively, but detects similar relative changes in the text. We find similar differences between the methods when looking at other novels; the NRC sentiment is high, the AFINN sentiment has more variance, and the Bing et al. sentiment appears to find longer stretches of similar text, but all three agree roughly on the overall trends in the sentiment through a narrative arc.

Why is, for example, the result for the NRC lexicon biased so high in sentiment compared to the Bing et al. result? Let's look briefly at how many positive and negative words are in these lexicons.

```
get_sentiments("nrc") %>%
    filter(sentiment %in% c("positive",
                            "negative")) %>%
  count(sentiment)

## # A tibble: 2 × 2
##   sentiment     n
##        <chr> <int>
## 1  negative  3324
## 2  positive  2312

get_sentiments("bing") %>%
  count(sentiment)

## # A tibble: 2 × 2
##   sentiment     n
##        <chr> <int>
## 1  negative  4782
## 2  positive  2006
```

Both lexicons have more negative than positive words, but the ratio of negative to positive words is higher in the Bing lexicon than the NRC lexicon. This will contribute to the effect we see in the plot above, as will any systematic difference in word matches, for example, if the negative words in the NRC lexicon do not match very well with the words that Jane Austen uses. Whatever the source of these differences, we see similar relative trajectories across the narrative arc, with similar changes in slope, but marked differences in absolute sentiment from lexicon to lexicon. This is important context to keep in mind when choosing a sentiment lexicon for analysis.

Most Common Positive and Negative Words

One advantage of having the data frame with both sentiment and word is that we can analyze word counts that contribute to each sentiment. By implementing count() here with arguments of both word and sentiment, we find out how much each word contributed to each sentiment.

```
bing_word_counts <- tidy_books %>%
  inner_join(get_sentiments("bing")) %>%
  count(word, sentiment, sort = TRUE) %>%
  ungroup()

bing_word_counts

## # A tibble: 2,585 × 3
##          word sentiment     n
##         <chr>     <chr> <int>
## 1       miss  negative  1855
## 2       well  positive  1523
## 3       good  positive  1380
## 4      great  positive   981
## 5       like  positive   725
## 6     better  positive   639
## 7     enough  positive   613
## 8      happy  positive   534
## 9       love  positive   495
## 10  pleasure  positive   462
## # ... with 2,575 more rows
```

This can be shown visually, and we can pipe straight into ggplot2, if we like, because of the way we are consistently using tools built for handling tidy data frames (Figure 2-4).

```
bing_word_counts %>%
  group_by(sentiment) %>%
  top_n(10) %>%
  ungroup() %>%
  mutate(word = reorder(word, n)) %>%
  ggplot(aes(word, n, fill = sentiment)) +
  geom_col(show.legend = FALSE) +
  facet_wrap(~sentiment, scales = "free_y") +
  labs(y = "Contribution to sentiment",
       x = NULL) +
  coord_flip()
```

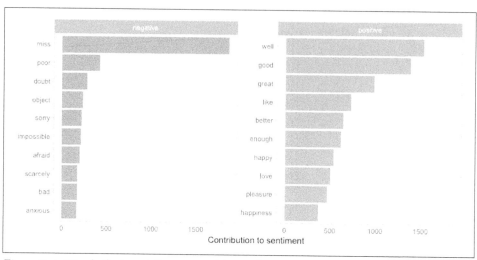

Contribution to sentiment

Figure 2-4. Words that contribute to positive and negative sentiment in Jane Austen's novels

Figure 2-4 lets us spot an anomaly in the sentiment analysis; the word "miss" is coded as negative but it is used as a title for young, unmarried women in Jane Austen's works. If it were appropriate for our purposes, we could easily add "miss" to a custom stop-words list using bind_rows(). We could implement that with a strategy such as this:

```
custom_stop_words <- bind_rows(data_frame(word = c("miss"),
                                          lexicon = c("custom")),
                               stop_words)

custom_stop_words
## # A tibble: 1,150 × 2
##            word lexicon
##           <chr>   <chr>
## 1          miss  custom
## 2             a   SMART
## 3           a's   SMART
## 4          able   SMART
## 5         about   SMART
## 6         above   SMART
## 7     according   SMART
## 8   accordingly   SMART
## 9        across   SMART
## 10      actually   SMART
## # ... with 1,140 more rows
```

Wordclouds

We've seen that this tidy text mining approach works well with ggplot2, but having our data in a tidy format is useful for other plots as well.

For example, consider the wordcloud package, which uses base R graphics. Let's look at the most common words in Jane Austen's works as a whole again, but this time as a wordcloud in Figure 2-5.

```
library(wordcloud)

tidy_books %>%
  anti_join(stop_words) %>%
  count(word) %>%
  with(wordcloud(word, n, max.words = 100))
```

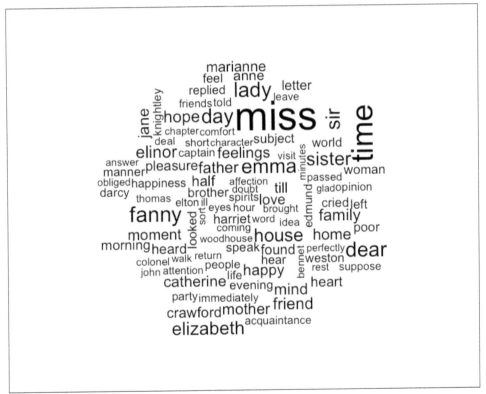

Figure 2-5. The most common words in Jane Austen's novels

In other functions, such as comparison.cloud(), you may need to turn the data frame into a matrix with reshape2's acast(). Let's do the sentiment analysis to tag positive and negative words using an inner join, then find the most common positive and negative words. Until the step where we need to send the data to compari son.cloud(), this can all be done with joins, piping, and dplyr because our data is in tidy format (Figure 2-6).

```
library(reshape2)

tidy_books %>%
  inner_join(get_sentiments("bing")) %>%
  count(word, sentiment, sort = TRUE) %>%
  acast(word ~ sentiment, value.var = "n", fill = 0) %>%
  comparison.cloud(colors = c("gray20", "gray80"),
                   max.words = 100)
```

Figure 2-6. Most common positive and negative words in Jane Austen's novels

The size of a word's text in Figure 2-6 is in proportion to its frequency within its sentiment. We can use this visualization to see the most important positive and negative words, but the sizes of the words are not comparable across sentiments.

Looking at Units Beyond Just Words

Lots of useful work can be done by tokenizing at the word level, but sometimes it is useful or necessary to look at different units of text. For example, some sentiment analysis algorithms look beyond only unigrams (i.e., single words) to try to understand the sentiment of a sentence as a whole. These algorithms try to understand that "I am not having a good day" is a sad sentence, not a happy one, because of negation. R packages including coreNLP (Arnold and Tilton 2016), cleanNLP (Arnold 2016), and sentimentr (Rinker 2017) are examples of such sentiment analysis algorithms. For these, we may want to tokenize text into sentences, and it makes sense to use a new name for the output column in such a case.

```
PandP_sentences <- data_frame(text = prideprejudice) %>%
    unnest_tokens(sentence, text, token = "sentences")
```

Let's look at just one.

```
PandP_sentences$sentence[2]

## [1] "however little known the feelings or views of such a man may be on his
first entering a neighbourhood, this truth is so well fixed in the minds of
the surrounding families, that he is considered the rightful property of some
one or other of their daughters."
```

The sentence tokenizing does seem to have a bit of trouble with UTF-8 encoded text, especially with sections of dialogue; it does much better with punctuation in ASCII. One possibility, if this is important, is to try using iconv() with something like iconv(text, to = 'latin1') in a mutate statement before unnesting.

Another option in unnest_tokens() is to split into tokens using a regex pattern. We could use this, for example, to split the text of Jane Austen's novels into a data frame by chapter.

```
austen_chapters <- austen_books() %>%
    group_by(book) %>%
    unnest_tokens(chapter, text, token = "regex",
                pattern = "Chapter|CHAPTER [\\dIVXLC]") %>%
    ungroup()

austen_chapters %>%
    group_by(book) %>%
    summarise(chapters = n())

## # A tibble: 6 × 2
##             book chapters
##            <fctr>    <int>
```

```
## 1 Sense & Sensibility          51
## 2    Pride & Prejudice         62
## 3      Mansfield Park          49
## 4                Emma          56
## 5   Northanger Abbey           32
## 6          Persuasion          25
```

We have recovered the correct number of chapters in each novel (plus an "extra" row for each novel title). In the `austen_chapters` data frame, each row corresponds to one chapter.

Near the beginning of this chapter, we used a similar regex to find where all the chapters were in Austen's novels for a tidy data frame organized by one word per row. We can use tidy text analysis to ask questions such as what are the most negative chapters in each of Jane Austen's novels? First, let's get the list of negative words from the Bing lexicon. Second, let's make a data frame of how many words are in each chapter so we can normalize for chapter length. Then, let's find the number of negative words in each chapter and divide by the total words in each chapter. For each book, which chapter has the highest proportion of negative words?

```
bingnegative <- get_sentiments("bing") %>%
  filter(sentiment == "negative")

wordcounts <- tidy_books %>%
  group_by(book, chapter) %>%
  summarize(words = n())

tidy_books %>%
  semi_join(bingnegative) %>%
  group_by(book, chapter) %>%
  summarize(negativewords = n()) %>%
  left_join(wordcounts, by = c("book", "chapter")) %>%
  mutate(ratio = negativewords/words) %>%
  filter(chapter != 0) %>%
  top_n(1) %>%
  ungroup()
```

```
## # A tibble: 6 × 5
##                   book chapter negativewords words      ratio
##                  <fctr>   <int>         <int> <int>      <dbl>
## 1 Sense & Sensibility      43           161  3405 0.04728341
## 2    Pride & Prejudice     34           111  2104 0.05275665
## 3      Mansfield Park      46           173  3685 0.04694708
## 4                Emma      15           151  3340 0.04520958
## 5   Northanger Abbey      21           149  2982 0.04996647
## 6          Persuasion       4            62  1807 0.03431101
```

These are the chapters with the most sad words in each book, normalized for number of words in the chapter. What is happening in these chapters? In Chapter 43 of *Sense and Sensibility*, Marianne is seriously ill, near death; and in Chapter 34 of *Pride and Prejudice*, Mr. Darcy proposes for the first time (so badly!). Chapter 46 of *Mansfield*

Park is almost the end, when everyone learns of Henry's scandalous adultery; Chapter 15 of *Emma* is when horrifying Mr. Elton proposes; and in Chapter 21 of *Northanger Abbey*, Catherine is deep in her Gothic faux fantasy of murder. Chapter 4 of *Persuasion* is when the reader gets the full flashback of Anne refusing Captain Wentworth, how sad she was, and what a terrible mistake she realized it to be.

Summary

Sentiment analysis provides a way to understand the attitudes and opinions expressed in texts. In this chapter, we explored how to approach sentiment analysis using tidy data principles; when text data is in a tidy data structure, sentiment analysis can be implemented as an inner join. We can use sentiment analysis to understand how a narrative arc changes throughout its course or what words with emotional and opinion content are important for a particular text. We will continue to develop our toolbox for applying sentiment analysis to different kinds of text in our case studies later in this book.

## CHAPTER 3

Analyzing Word and Document Frequency: tf-idf

A central question in text mining and natural language processing is how to quantify what a document is about. Can we do this by looking at the words that make up the document? One measure of how important a word may be is its *term frequency* (tf), how frequently a word occurs in a document, as we examined in Chapter 1. There are words in a document, however, that occur many times but may not be important; in English, these are probably words like "the," "is," "of," and so forth. We might take the approach of adding words like these to a list of stop words and removing them before analysis, but it is possible that some of these words might be more important in some documents than others. A list of stop words is not a very sophisticated approach to adjusting term frequency for commonly used words.

Another approach is to look at a term's *inverse document frequency* (idf), which decreases the weight for commonly used words and increases the weight for words that are not used very much in a collection of documents. This can be combined with term frequency to calculate a term's *tf-idf* (the two quantities multiplied together), the frequency of a term adjusted for how rarely it is used.

The statistic tf-idf is intended to measure how important a word is to a document in a collection (or corpus) of documents, for example, to one novel in a collection of novels or to one website in a collection of websites.

The statistic tf-idf is a rule of thumb or heuristic quantity; while it has proved useful in text mining, search engines, etc., its theoretical foundations are considered less than firm by information theory experts. The inverse document frequency for any given term is defined as:

$$idf(\text{term}) = \ln\left(\frac{n_{\text{documents}}}{n_{\text{documents containing term}}}\right)$$

We can use tidy data principles, as described in Chapter 1, to approach tf-idf analysis and use consistent, effective tools to quantify how important various terms are in a document that is part of a collection.

Term Frequency in Jane Austen's Novels

Let's start by looking at the published novels of Jane Austen and first examine term frequency, then tf-idf. We can start just by using dplyr verbs such as `group_by()` and `join()`. What are the most commonly used words in Jane Austen's novels? (Let's also calculate the total words in each novel here, for later use.)

```
library(dplyr)
library(janeaustenr)
library(tidytext)

book_words <- austen_books() %>%
  unnest_tokens(word, text) %>%
  count(book, word, sort = TRUE) %>%
  ungroup()

total_words <- book_words %>%
  group_by(book) %>%
  summarize(total = sum(n))

book_words <- left_join(book_words, total_words)

book_words

## # A tibble: 40,379 x 4
##                     book  word     n  total
##                   <fctr> <chr> <int>  <int>
## 1        Mansfield Park   the  6206 160460
## 2        Mansfield Park    to  5475 160460
## 3        Mansfield Park   and  5438 160460
## 4                  Emma    to  5239 160996
## 5                  Emma   the  5201 160996
## 6                  Emma   and  4896 160996
## 7        Mansfield Park    of  4778 160460
## 8     Pride & Prejudice   the  4331 122204
## 9                  Emma    of  4291 160996
## 10    Pride & Prejudice    to  4162 122204
## # ... with 40,369 more rows
```

There is one row in this `book_words` data frame for each word-book combination; n is the number of times that word is used in that book, and `total` is the total number of words in that book. The usual suspects are here with the highest n, "the," "and," "to," and so forth. In Figure 3-1, let's look at the distribution of n/total for each novel: the number of times a word appears in a novel divided by the total number of terms (words) in that novel. This is exactly what term frequency is.

```
library(ggplot2)

ggplot(book_words, aes(n/total, fill = book)) +
  geom_histogram(show.legend = FALSE) +
  xlim(NA, 0.0009) +
  facet_wrap(~book, ncol = 2, scales = "free_y")
```

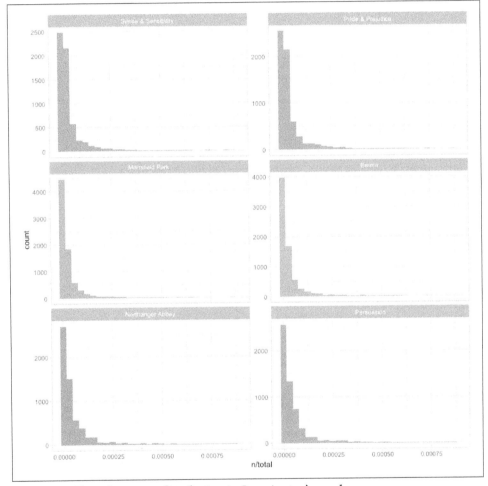

Figure 3-1. Term frequency distribution in Jane Austen's novels

There are very long tails to the right for these novels (those extremely common words!) that we have not shown in these plots. These plots exhibit similar distributions for all the novels, with many words that occur rarely and fewer words that occur frequently.

Zipf's Law

Distributions like those shown in Figure 3-1 are typical in language. In fact, those types of long-tailed distributions are so common in any given corpus of natural language (like a book, or a lot of text from a website, or spoken words) that the relationship between the frequency that a word is used and its rank has been the subject of study. A classic version of this relationship is called Zipf's law, after George Zipf, a 20th-century American linguist.

Zipf's law states that the frequency that a word appears is inversely proportional to its rank.

Since we have the data frame we used to plot term frequency, we can examine Zipf's law for Jane Austen's novels with just a few lines of dplyr functions.

```
freq_by_rank <- book_words %>%
  group_by(book) %>%
  mutate(rank = row_number(),
         `term frequency` = n/total)

freq_by_rank

## Source: local data frame [40,379 x 6]
## Groups: book [6]
##
##                  book  word     n  total  rank `term frequency`
##                 <fctr> <chr> <int>  <int> <int>            <dbl>
## 1       Mansfield Park   the  6206 160460     1       0.03867631
## 2       Mansfield Park    to  5475 160460     2       0.03412065
## 3       Mansfield Park   and  5438 160460     3       0.03389007
## 4                 Emma    to  5239 160996     1       0.03254118
## 5                 Emma   the  5201 160996     2       0.03230515
## 6                 Emma   and  4896 160996     3       0.03041069
## 7       Mansfield Park    of  4778 160460     4       0.02977689
## 8    Pride & Prejudice   the  4331 122204     1       0.03544074
## 9                 Emma    of  4291 160996     4       0.02665284
## 10   Pride & Prejudice    to  4162 122204     2       0.03405780
## # ... with 40,369 more rows
```

The rank column here tells us the rank of each word within the frequency table; the table was already ordered by n, so we could use row_number() to find the rank. Then, we can calculate the term frequency in the same way we did before. Zipf's law is often visualized by plotting rank on the x-axis and term frequency on the y-axis, on logarithmic scales. Plotting this way, an inversely proportional relationship will have a constant, negative slope (Figure 3-2).

```
freq_by_rank %>%
  ggplot(aes(rank, `term frequency`, color = book)) +
  geom_line(size = 1.1, alpha = 0.8, show.legend = FALSE) +
  scale_x_log10() +
  scale_y_log10()
```

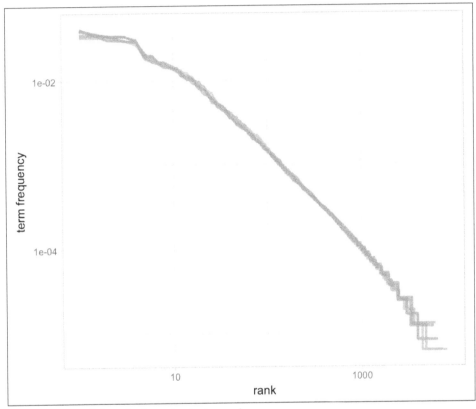

Figure 3-2. Zipf's law for Jane Austen's novels

Notice that Figure 3-2 is in log-log coordinates. We see that all six of Jane Austen's novels are similar to each other, and that the relationship between rank and frequency does have negative slope. It is not quite constant, though; perhaps we could view this as a broken power law (*https://en.wikipedia.org/wiki/Power_law*) with, say, three sections. Let's see what the exponent of the power law is for the middle section of the rank range.

```
rank_subset <- freq_by_rank %>%
  filter(rank < 500,
         rank > 10)
```

```
lm(log10(`term frequency`) ~ log10(rank), data = rank_subset)

##
## Call:
## lm(formula = log10(`term frequency`) ~ log10(rank), data = rank_subset)
##
## Coefficients:
## (Intercept)  log10(rank)
##     -0.6225      -1.1125
```

Classic versions of Zipf's law have frequency $\propto \frac{1}{\text{rank}}$ and we have in fact gotten a slope close to −1 here. Let's plot this fitted power law with the data in Figure 3-3 to see how it looks.

```
freq_by_rank %>%
  ggplot(aes(rank, `term frequency`, color = book)) +
  geom_abline(intercept = -0.62, slope = -1.1, color = "gray50", linetype = 2) +
  geom_line(size = 1.1, alpha = 0.8, show.legend = FALSE) +
  scale_x_log10() +
  scale_y_log10()
```

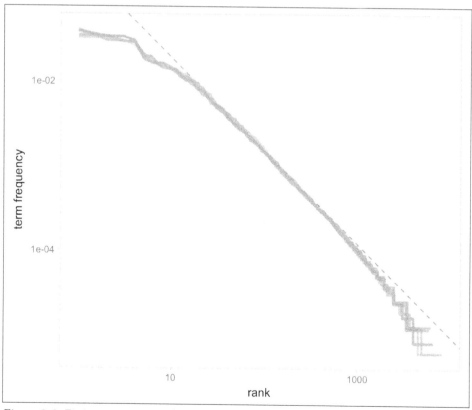

Figure 3-3. Fitting an exponent for Zipf's law with Jane Austen's novels

We have found a result close to the classic version of Zipf's law for the corpus of Jane Austen's novels. The deviations we see here at high rank are not uncommon for many kinds of language; a corpus of language often contains fewer rare words than predicted by a single power law. The deviations at low rank are more unusual. Jane Austen uses a lower percentage of the most common words than many collections of language. This kind of analysis could be extended to compare authors, or to compare any other collections of text; it can be implemented simply using tidy data principles.

The bind_tf_idf Function

The idea of tf-idf is to find the important words for the content of each document by decreasing the weight for commonly used words and increasing the weight for words that are not used very much in a collection or corpus of documents, in this case, the group of Jane Austen's novels as a whole. Calculating tf-idf attempts to find the words that are important (i.e., common) in a text, but not *too* common. Let's do that now.

The bind_tf_idf function in the tidytext package takes a tidy text dataset as input with one row per token (term), per document. One column (word here) contains the terms/tokens, one column contains the documents (book in this case), and the last necessary column contains the counts, or how many times each document contains each term (n in this example). We calculated a total for each book for our explorations in previous sections, but it is not necessary for the bind_tf_idf function; the table only needs to contain all the words in each document.

```
book_words <- book_words %>%
  bind_tf_idf(word, book, n)
book_words
```

```
## # A tibble: 40,379 × 7
##                book  word     n  total         tf   idf tf_idf
##              <fctr> <chr> <int>  <int>      <dbl> <dbl>  <dbl>
## 1    Mansfield Park   the  6206 160460 0.03867631     0      0
## 2    Mansfield Park    to  5475 160460 0.03412065     0      0
## 3    Mansfield Park   and  5438 160460 0.03389007     0      0
## 4              Emma    to  5239 160996 0.03254118     0      0
## 5              Emma   the  5201 160996 0.03230515     0      0
## 6              Emma   and  4896 160996 0.03041069     0      0
## 7    Mansfield Park    of  4778 160460 0.02977689     0      0
## 8  Pride & Prejudice  the  4331 122204 0.03544074     0      0
## 9              Emma    of  4291 160996 0.02665284     0      0
## 10 Pride & Prejudice   to  4162 122204 0.03405780     0      0
## # ... with 40,369 more rows
```

Notice that idf and thus tf-idf are zero for these extremely common words. These are all words that appear in all six of Jane Austen's novels, so the idf term (which will then be the natural log of 1) is zero. The inverse document frequency (and thus tf-idf) is very low (near zero) for words that occur in many of the documents in a collection;

this is how this approach decreases the weight for common words. The inverse document frequency will be a higher number for words that occur in fewer of the documents in the collection.

Let's look at terms with high tf-idf in Jane Austen's works.

```
book_words %>%
  select(-total) %>%
  arrange(desc(tf_idf))
```

```
## # A tibble: 40,379 × 6
##                    book     word     n          tf       idf      tf_idf
##                   <fctr>    <chr> <int>       <dbl>     <dbl>       <dbl>
## 1  Sense & Sensibility    elinor   623 0.005193528 1.791759 0.009305552
## 2  Sense & Sensibility   marianne  492 0.004101470 1.791759 0.007348847
## 3       Mansfield Park   crawford   493 0.003072417 1.791759 0.005505032
## 4      Pride & Prejudice    darcy   373 0.003052273 1.791759 0.005468939
## 5           Persuasion    elliot   254 0.003036207 1.791759 0.005440153
## 6                 Emma      emma   786 0.004882109 1.098612 0.005363545
## 7     Northanger Abbey    tilney   196 0.002519928 1.791759 0.004515105
## 8                 Emma    weston   389 0.002416209 1.791759 0.004329266
## 9      Pride & Prejudice   bennet  294 0.002405813 1.791759 0.004310639
## 10          Persuasion wentworth  191 0.002283132 1.791759 0.004090824
## # ... with 40,369 more rows
```

Here we see all proper nouns, names that are in fact important in these novels. None of them occur in all of the novels, and they are important, characteristic words for each text within the corpus of Jane Austen's novels.

Some of the values for idf are the same for different terms because there are six documents in this corpus and we are seeing the numerical value for ln(6/1), ln(6/2), etc.

Let's look at a visualization for these high tf-idf words in Figure 3-4.

```
book_words %>%
  arrange(desc(tf_idf)) %>%
  mutate(word = factor(word, levels = rev(unique(word)))) %>%
  group_by(book) %>%
  top_n(15) %>%
  ungroup %>%
  ggplot(aes(word, tf_idf, fill = book)) +
  geom_col(show.legend = FALSE) +
  labs(x = NULL, y = "tf-idf") +
  facet_wrap(~book, ncol = 2, scales = "free") +
  coord_flip()
```

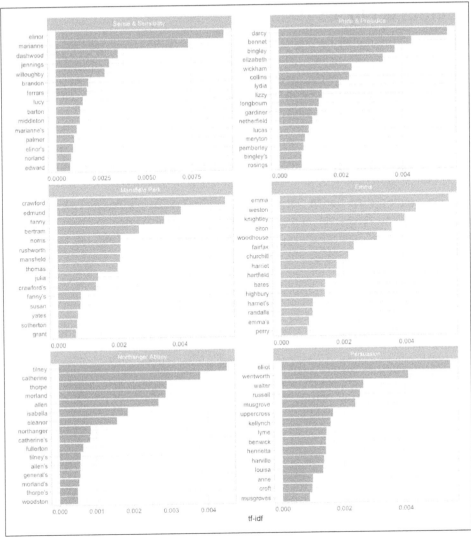

Figure 3-4. Highest tf-idf words in each of Jane Austen's novels

Still all proper nouns in Figure 3-4! These words are, as measured by tf-idf, the most important to each novel and most readers would likely agree. What measuring tf-idf has done here is show us that Jane Austen used similar language across her six novels, and what distinguishes one novel from the rest within the collection of her works are the proper nouns, the names of people and places. This is the point of tf-idf; it identifies words that are important to one document within a collection of documents.

A Corpus of Physics Texts

Let's work with another corpus of documents to see what terms are important in a different set of works. In fact, let's leave the world of fiction and narrative entirely. Let's download some classic physics texts from Project Gutenberg and see what terms are important in these works, as measured by tf-idf. Let's download *Discourse on Floating Bodies* by Galileo Galilei (*http://www.gutenberg.org/ebooks/37729*), *Treatise on Light* by Christiaan Huygens (*http://www.gutenberg.org/ebooks/14725*), *Experiments with Alternate Currents of High Potential and High Frequency* by Nikola Tesla (*http://www.gutenberg.org/ebooks/13476*), and *Relativity: The Special and General Theory* by Albert Einstein (*http://www.gutenberg.org/ebooks/5001*).

This is a pretty diverse bunch. They may all be physics classics, but they were written across a 300-year time span, and some of them were first written in other languages and then translated to English. Perfectly homogeneous these are not, but that doesn't stop this from being an interesting exercise!

```
library(gutenbergr)
physics <- gutenberg_download(c(37729, 14725, 13476, 5001),
                              meta_fields = "author")
```

Now that we have the texts, let's use `unnest_tokens()` and `count()` to find out how many times each word is used in each text.

```
physics_words <- physics %>%
  unnest_tokens(word, text) %>%
  count(author, word, sort = TRUE) %>%
  ungroup()

physics_words

## # A tibble: 12,592 × 3
##                      author  word     n
##                       <chr> <chr> <int>
## 1       Galilei, Galileo     the  3760
## 2         Tesla, Nikola      the  3604
## 3   Huygens, Christiaan      the  3553
## 4       Einstein, Albert     the  2994
## 5       Galilei, Galileo      of  2049
## 6       Einstein, Albert      of  2030
## 7         Tesla, Nikola       of  1737
## 8   Huygens, Christiaan       of  1708
## 9   Huygens, Christiaan       to  1207
## 10        Tesla, Nikola        a  1176
## # ... with 12,582 more rows
```

Here we see just the raw counts; we need to remember that these documents are all different lengths. Let's go ahead and calculate tf-idf, then visualize the high tf-idf words in Figure 3-5.

```
plot_physics <- physics_words %>%
  bind_tf_idf(word, author, n) %>%
  arrange(desc(tf_idf)) %>%
  mutate(word = factor(word, levels = rev(unique(word)))) %>%
  mutate(author = factor(author, levels = c("Galilei, Galileo",
                                            "Huygens, Christiaan",
                                            "Tesla, Nikola",
                                            "Einstein, Albert")))

plot_physics %>%
  group_by(author) %>%
  top_n(15, tf_idf) %>%
  ungroup() %>%
  mutate(word = reorder(word, tf_idf)) %>%
  ggplot(aes(word, tf_idf, fill = author)) +
  geom_col(show.legend = FALSE) +
  labs(x = NULL, y = "tf-idf") +
  facet_wrap(~author, ncol = 2, scales = "free") +
  coord_flip()
```

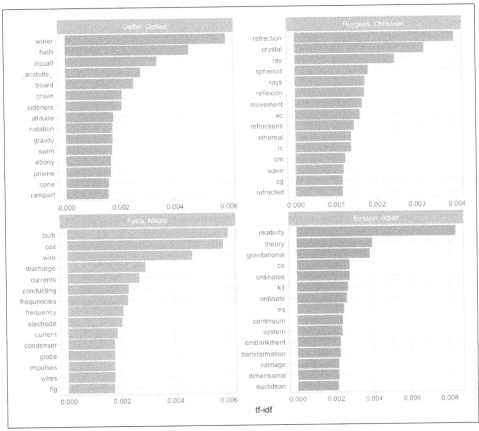

Figure 3-5. Highest tf-idf words in each physics text

Very interesting indeed. One thing we see here is "eq" in the Einstein text?!

```
library(stringr)

physics %>%
  filter(str_detect(text, "eq\\.")) %>%
  select(text)
```

```
## # A tibble: 55 × 1
##                                                               text
##                                                              <chr>
## 1                                         eq. 1: file eq01.gif
## 2                                         eq. 2: file eq02.gif
## 3                                         eq. 3: file eq03.gif
## 4                                         eq. 4: file eq04.gif
## 5                                       eq. 05a: file eq05a.gif
## 6                                       eq. 05b: file eq05b.gif
## 7                      the distance between the points being eq. 06 .
## 8   direction of its length with a velocity v is eq. 06 of a metre.
## 9                            velocity v=c we should have eq. 06a ,
## 10            the rod as judged from K1 would have been eq. 06 ;
## # ... with 45 more rows
```

Some cleaning up of the text may be in order. "K1" is the name of a coordinate system for Einstein:

```
physics %>%
  filter(str_detect(text, "K1")) %>%
  select(text)
```

```
## # A tibble: 59 × 1
##                                                               text
##                                                              <chr>
## 1          to a second co-ordinate system K1 provided that the latter is
## 2          condition of uniform motion of translation. Relative to K1 the
## 3      tenet thus: If, relative to K, K1 is a uniformly moving co-ordinate
## 4     with respect to K1 according to exactly the same general laws as with
## 5   does not hold, then the Galilean co-ordinate systems K, K1, K2, etc.,
## 6    Relative to K1, the same event would be fixed in respect of space and
## 7    to K1, when the magnitudes x, y, z, t, of the same event with respect
## 8     of light (and of course for every ray) with respect to K and K1. For
## 9   reference-body K and for the reference-body K1. A light-signal is sent
## 10  immediately follows. If referred to the system K1, the propagation of
## # ... with 49 more rows
```

Maybe it makes sense to keep this one. Also notice that in this line we have "co-ordinate," which explains why there are separate "co" and "ordinate" items in the high tf-idf words for the Einstein text; the unnest_tokens() function separates around punctuation. Notice that the tf-idf scores for "co" and "ordinate" are close to the same!

"AB," "RC," and so forth are names of rays, circles, angles, and so on for Huygens:

```
physics %>%
  filter(str_detect(text, "AK")) %>%
  select(text)
```

```
## # A tibble: 34 × 1
##                                                                        text
##                                                                       <chr>
##  1   Now let us assume that the ray has come from A to C along AK, KC; the
##  2    be equal to the time along KMN. But the time along AK is longer than
##  3  that along AL: hence the time along AKN is longer than that along ABC.
##  4      And KC being longer than KN, the time along AKC will exceed, by as
##  5      line which is comprised between the perpendiculars AK, BL. Then it
##  6  ordinary refraction. Now it appears that AK and BL dip down toward the
##  7  side where the air is less easy to penetrate: for AK being longer than
##  8     than do AK, BL. And this suffices to show that the ray will continue
##  9      surface AB at the points AK_k_B. Then instead of the hemispherical
## 10  along AL, LB, and along AK, KB, are always represented by the line AH,
## # ... with 24 more rows
```

Let's remove some of these less meaningful words to make a better, more meaningful plot. Notice that we make a custom list of stop words and use `anti_join()` to remove them; this is a flexible approach that can be used in many situations. We will need to go back a few steps since we are removing words from the tidy data frame (Figure 3-6).

```
mystopwords <- data_frame(word = c("eq", "co", "rc", "ac", "ak", "bn",
                                   "fig", "file", "cg", "cb", "cm"))
physics_words <- anti_join(physics_words, mystopwords, by = "word")
plot_physics <- physics_words %>%
  bind_tf_idf(word, author, n) %>%
  arrange(desc(tf_idf)) %>%
  mutate(word = factor(word, levels = rev(unique(word)))) %>%
  group_by(author) %>%
  top_n(15, tf_idf) %>%
  ungroup %>%
  mutate(author = factor(author, levels = c("Galilei, Galileo",
                                            "Huygens, Christiaan",
                                            "Tesla, Nikola",
                                            "Einstein, Albert")))

ggplot(plot_physics, aes(word, tf_idf, fill = author)) +
  geom_col(show.legend = FALSE) +
  labs(x = NULL, y = "tf-idf") +
  facet_wrap(~author, ncol = 2, scales = "free") +
  coord_flip()
```

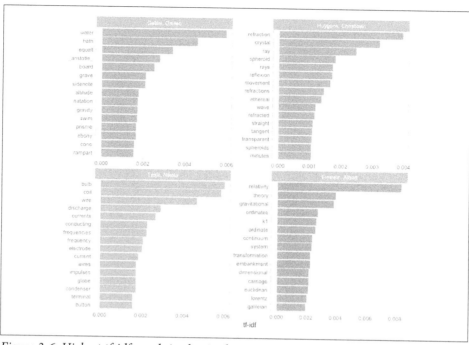

Figure 3-6. Highest tf-idf words in classic physics texts

One thing we can conclude from Figure 3-6 is that we don't hear enough about ramparts or things being ethereal in physics today.

Summary

Using term frequency and inverse document frequency allows us to find words that are characteristic for one document within a collection of documents, whether that document is a novel or physics text or webpage. Exploring term frequency on its own can give us insight into how language is used in a collection of natural language, and dplyr verbs like `count()` and `rank()` give us tools to reason about term frequency. The tidytext package uses an implementation of tf-idf consistent with tidy data principles that enables us to see how different words are important in documents within a collection or corpus of documents.

## CHAPTER 4

Relationships Between Words: N-grams and Correlations

So far we've considered words as individual units, and considered their relationships to sentiments or to documents. However, many interesting text analyses are based on the relationships between words, whether examining which words tend to follow others immediately, or words that tend to co-occur within the same documents.

In this chapter, we'll explore some of the methods tidytext offers for calculating and visualizing relationships between words in your text dataset. This includes the token = "ngrams" argument, which tokenizes by pairs of adjacent words rather than by individual ones. We'll also introduce two new packages: ggraph (*https://github.com/thomasp85/ggraph*), by Thomas Pedersen, which extends ggplot2 to construct network plots, and widyr (*https://github.com/dgrtwo/widyr*), which calculates pairwise correlations and distances within a tidy data frame. Together these expand our toolbox for exploring text within the tidy data framework.

Tokenizing by N-gram

We've been using the unnest_tokens function to tokenize by word, or sometimes by sentence, which is useful for the kinds of sentiment and frequency analyses we've been doing so far. But we can also use the function to tokenize into consecutive sequences of words, called *n-grams*. By seeing how often word X is followed by word Y, we can then build a model of the relationships between them.

We do this by adding the token = "ngrams" option to unnest_tokens(), and setting n to the number of words we wish to capture in each n-gram. When we set n to 2, we are examining pairs of two consecutive words, often called "bigrams":

```
library(dplyr)
library(tidytext)
library(janeaustenr)

austen_bigrams <- austen_books() %>%
  unnest_tokens(bigram, text, token = "ngrams", n = 2)

austen_bigrams
```

```
## # A tibble: 725,048 × 2
##                   book           bigram
##                  <fctr>           <chr>
## 1  Sense & Sensibility        sense and
## 2  Sense & Sensibility  and sensibility
## 3  Sense & Sensibility   sensibility by
## 4  Sense & Sensibility          by jane
## 5  Sense & Sensibility      jane austen
## 6  Sense & Sensibility      austen 1811
## 7  Sense & Sensibility     1811 chapter
## 8  Sense & Sensibility        chapter 1
## 9  Sense & Sensibility            1 the
## 10 Sense & Sensibility       the family
## # ... with 725,038 more rows
```

This data structure is still a variation of the tidy text format. It is structured as one token per row (with extra metadata, such as book, still preserved), but each token now represents a bigram.

Notice that these bigrams overlap: "sense and" is one token, while "and sensibility" is another.

Counting and Filtering N-grams

Our usual tidy tools apply equally well to n-gram analysis. We can examine the most common bigrams using dplyr's count():

```
austen_bigrams %>%
  count(bigram, sort = TRUE)
```

```
## # A tibble: 211,237 × 2
##      bigram     n
##       <chr> <int>
## 1    of the  3017
## 2     to be  2787
## 3    in the  2368
## 4    it was  1781
## 5      i am  1545
## 6   she had  1472
## 7    of her  1445
```

```
## 8      to the  1387
## 9    she was  1377
## 10  had been  1299
## # ... with 211,227 more rows
```

As one might expect, a lot of the most common bigrams are pairs of common (uninteresting) words, such as "of the" and "to be," what we call "stop words" (see Chapter 1). This is a useful time to use tidyr's `separate()`, which splits a column into multiple columns based on a delimiter. This lets us separate it into two columns, "word1" and "word2," at which point we can remove cases where either is a stop word.

```
library(tidyr)

bigrams_separated <- austen_bigrams %>%
  separate(bigram, c("word1", "word2"), sep = " ")

bigrams_filtered <- bigrams_separated %>%
  filter(!word1 %in% stop_words$word) %>%
  filter(!word2 %in% stop_words$word)

# new bigram counts:
bigram_counts <- bigrams_filtered %>%
  count(word1, word2, sort = TRUE)

bigram_counts

## Source: local data frame [33,421 x 3]
## Groups: word1 [6,711]
##
##         word1      word2      n
##         <chr>      <chr>  <int>
## 1         sir     thomas    287
## 2        miss   crawford    215
## 3     captain  wentworth    170
## 4        miss  woodhouse    162
## 5       frank  churchill    132
## 6        lady    russell    118
## 7        lady    bertram    114
## 8         sir     walter    113
## 9        miss    fairfax    109
## 10    colonel    brandon    108
## # ... with 33,411 more rows
```

We can see that names (whether first and last or with a salutation) are the most common pairs in Jane Austen books.

In other analyses, we may want to work with the recombined words. tidyr's `unite()` function is the inverse of `separate()`, and lets us recombine the columns into one. Thus, "separate/filter/count/unite" let us find the most common bigrams not containing stop words.

```
bigrams_united <- bigrams_filtered %>%
  unite(bigram, word1, word2, sep = " ")

bigrams_united

## # A tibble: 44,784 × 2
##                   book              bigram
## *                <fctr>               <chr>
## 1  Sense & Sensibility         jane austen
## 2  Sense & Sensibility         austen 1811
## 3  Sense & Sensibility        1811 chapter
## 4  Sense & Sensibility           chapter 1
## 5  Sense & Sensibility        norland park
## 6  Sense & Sensibility surrounding acquaintance
## 7  Sense & Sensibility          late owner
## 8  Sense & Sensibility        advanced age
## 9  Sense & Sensibility   constant companion
## 10 Sense & Sensibility        happened ten
## # ... with 44,774 more rows
```

In other analyses you may be interested in the most common trigrams, which are consecutive sequences of three words. We can find this by setting n = 3.

```
austen_books() %>%
  unnest_tokens(trigram, text, token = "ngrams", n = 3) %>%
  separate(trigram, c("word1", "word2", "word3"), sep = " ") %>%
  filter(!word1 %in% stop_words$word,
         !word2 %in% stop_words$word,
         !word3 %in% stop_words$word) %>%
  count(word1, word2, word3, sort = TRUE)

## Source: local data frame [8,757 x 4]
## Groups: word1, word2 [7,462]
##
##        word1     word2     word3     n
##        <chr>     <chr>     <chr> <int>
## 1       dear      miss woodhouse    23
## 2       miss        de   bourgh    18
## 3       lady catherine        de    14
## 4  catherine        de   bourgh    13
## 5       poor      miss    taylor    11
## 6        sir    walter    elliot    11
## 7        ten  thousand    pounds    11
## 8       dear       sir    thomas    10
## 9     twenty  thousand    pounds     8
## 10   replied      miss  crawford     7
## # ... with 8,747 more rows
```

Analyzing Bigrams

This one-bigram-per-row format is helpful for exploratory analyses of the text. As a simple example, we might be interested in the most common "streets" mentioned in each book.

```
bigrams_filtered %>%
  filter(word2 == "street") %>%
  count(book, word1, sort = TRUE)

## Source: local data frame [34 x 3]
## Groups: book [6]
##
##                    book        word1      n
##                  <fctr>        <chr>  <int>
## 1  Sense & Sensibility      berkeley     16
## 2  Sense & Sensibility        harley     16
## 3     Northanger Abbey      pulteney     14
## 4     Northanger Abbey        milsom     11
## 5       Mansfield Park       wimpole     10
## 6    Pride & Prejudice  gracechurch      9
## 7  Sense & Sensibility       conduit      6
## 8  Sense & Sensibility          bond      5
## 9           Persuasion        milsom      5
## 10          Persuasion        rivers      4
## # ... with 24 more rows
```

A bigram can also be treated as a term in a document in the same way that we treated individual words. For example, we can look at the tf-idf (Chapter 3) of bigrams across Austen novels. These tf-idf values can be visualized within each book, just as we did for words (Figure 4-1).

```
bigram_tf_idf <- bigrams_united %>%
  count(book, bigram) %>%
  bind_tf_idf(bigram, book, n) %>%
  arrange(desc(tf_idf))

bigram_tf_idf

## Source: local data frame [36,217 x 6]
## Groups: book [6]
##
##                    book            bigram      n         tf        idf     tf_idf
##                  <fctr>             <chr>  <int>      <dbl>      <dbl>      <dbl>
## 1           Persuasion  captain wentworth    170 0.02985599 1.791759 0.05349475
## 2       Mansfield Park        sir thomas    287 0.02873160 1.791759 0.05148012
## 3       Mansfield Park     miss crawford    215 0.02152368 1.791759 0.03856525
## 4           Persuasion      lady russell    118 0.02072357 1.791759 0.03713165
## 5           Persuasion        sir walter    113 0.01984545 1.791759 0.03555828
## 6                 Emma    miss woodhouse    162 0.01700966 1.791759 0.03047722
## 7     Northanger Abbey       miss tilney     82 0.01594400 1.791759 0.02856782
## 8  Sense & Sensibility   colonel brandon    108 0.01502086 1.791759 0.02691377
## 9                 Emma   frank churchill    132 0.01385972 1.791759 0.02483329
## 10   Pride & Prejudice    lady catherine    100 0.01380453 1.791759 0.02473439
## # ... with 36,207 more rows
```

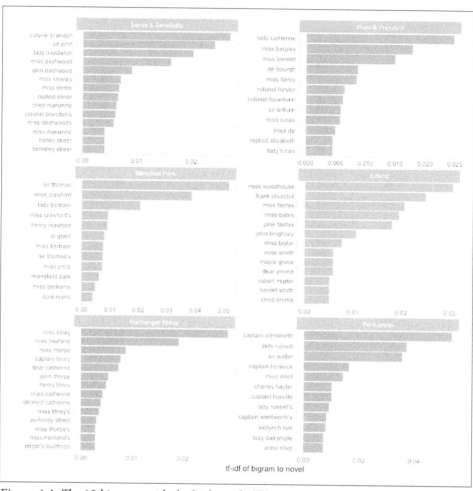

Figure 4-1. The 12 bigrams with the highest tf-idf from each Jane Austen novel

Much as we discovered in Chapter 3, the units that distinguish each Austen book are almost exclusively names. We also notice some pairings of a common verb and a name, such as "replied elizabeth" in *Pride and Prejudice*, or "cried emma" in *Emma*.

There are advantages and disadvantages to examining the tf-idf of bigrams rather than individual words. Pairs of consecutive words might capture structure that isn't present when one is just counting single words, and may provide context that makes tokens more understandable (for example, "pulteney street," in *Northanger Abbey*, is more informative than "pulteney"). However, the per-bigram counts are also *sparser*: a typical two-word pair is rarer than either of its component words. Thus, bigrams can be especially useful when you have a very large text dataset.

Using Bigrams to Provide Context in Sentiment Analysis

Our sentiment analysis approch in Chapter 2 simply counted the appearance of positive or negative words, according to a reference lexicon. One of the problems with this approach is that a word's context can matter nearly as much as its presence. For example, the words "happy" and "like" will be counted as positive, even in a sentence like "I'm not **happy** and I don't **like** it!"

Now that we have the data organized into bigrams, it's easy to tell how often words are preceded by a word like "not."

```
bigrams_separated %>%
  filter(word1 == "not") %>%
  count(word1, word2, sort = TRUE)

## Source: local data frame [1,246 x 3]
## Groups: word1 [1]
##
##     word1 word2      n
##     <chr> <chr>  <int>
## 1    not     be    610
## 2    not     to    355
## 3    not   have    327
## 4    not   know    252
## 5    not      a    189
## 6    not  think    176
## 7    not   been    160
## 8    not    the    147
## 9    not     at    129
## 10   not     in    118
## # ... with 1,236 more rows
```

By performing sentiment analysis on the bigram data, we can examine how often sentiment-associated words are preceded by "not" or other negating words. We could use this to ignore or even reverse their contribution to the sentiment score.

Let's use the AFINN lexicon for sentiment analysis, which you may recall gives a numeric sentiment score for each word, with positive or negative numbers indicating the direction of the sentiment.

```
AFINN <- get_sentiments("afinn")

AFINN

## # A tibble: 2,476 x 2
##         word score
##        <chr> <int>
## 1    abandon    -2
## 2  abandoned    -2
## 3   abandons    -2
## 4   abducted    -2
## 5  abduction    -2
```

```
## 6    abductions    -2
## 7          abhor    -3
## 8       abhorred    -3
## 9      abhorrent    -3
## 10        abhors    -3
## # ... with 2,466 more rows
```

We can then examine the most frequent words that were preceded by "not" and were associated with a sentiment.

```
not_words <- bigrams_separated %>%
  filter(word1 == "not") %>%
  inner_join(AFINN, by = c(word2 = "word")) %>%
  count(word2, score, sort = TRUE) %>%
  ungroup()

not_words
```

```
## # A tibble: 245 × 3
##       word2 score       n
##       <chr> <int> <int>
## 1      like     2    99
## 2      help     2    82
## 3      want     1    45
## 4      wish     1    39
## 5     allow     1    36
## 6      care     2    23
## 7     sorry    -1    21
## 8     leave    -1    18
## 9   pretend    -1    18
## 10    worth     2    17
## # ... with 235 more rows
```

For example, the most common sentiment-associated word to follow "not" was "like," which would normally have a (positive) score of 2.

It's worth asking which words contributed the most in the "wrong" direction. To compute that, we can multiply their score by the number of times they appear (so that a word with a score of +3 occurring 10 times has as much impact as a word with a sentiment score of +1 occurring 30 times). We visualize the result with a bar plot (Figure 4-2).

```
not_words %>%
  mutate(contribution = n * score) %>%
  arrange(desc(abs(contribution))) %>%
  head(20) %>%
  mutate(word2 = reorder(word2, contribution)) %>%
  ggplot(aes(word2, n * score, fill = n * score > 0)) +
  geom_col(show.legend = FALSE) +
  xlab("Words preceded by \"not\"") +
  ylab("Sentiment score * number of occurrences") +
  coord_flip()
```

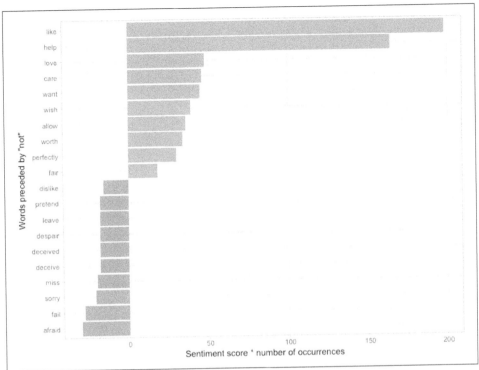

Figure 4-2. The 20 words followed by "not" that had the greatest contribution to sentiment scores, in either a positive or negative direction

The bigrams "not like" and "not help" were overwhelmingly the largest causes of misidentification, making the text seem much more positive than it is. But we can see that phrases like "not afraid" and "not fail" sometimes suggest text is more negative than it is.

"Not" isn't the only term that provides some context for the following word. We could pick four common words (or more) that negate the subsequent term, and use the same joining and counting approach to examine all of them at once.

```
negation_words <- c("not", "no", "never", "without")

negated_words <- bigrams_separated %>%
  filter(word1 %in% negation_words) %>%
  inner_join(AFINN, by = c(word2 = "word")) %>%
  count(word1, word2, score, sort = TRUE) %>%
  ungroup()
```

We could then visualize what the most common words to follow each particular negation are (Figure 4-3). While "not like" and "not help" are still the two most common examples, we can also see pairings such as "no great" and "never loved." We could combine this with the approaches in Chapter 2 to reverse the AFINN scores of each word that follows a negation. These are just a few examples of how finding consecutive words can give context to text mining methods.

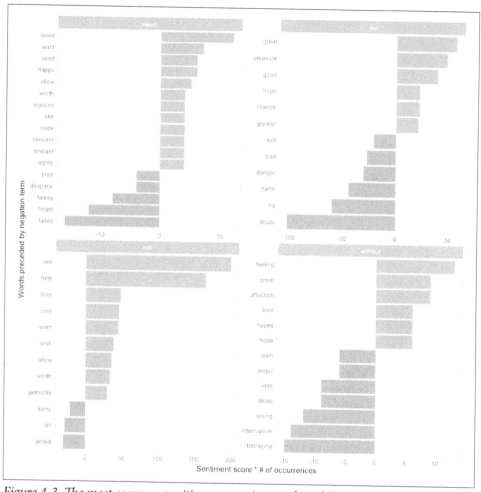

Figure 4-3. The most common positive or negative words to follow negations such as "never," "no," "not," and "without"

Visualizing a Network of Bigrams with ggraph

We may be interested in visualizing all of the relationships among words simultaneously, rather than just the top few at a time. As one common visualization, we can arrange the words into a network, or "graph." Here we'll be referring to a graph not in the sense of a visualization, but as a combination of connected nodes. A graph can be constructed from a tidy object since it has three variables:

from

> The node an edge is coming from

to

> The node an edge is going toward

weight

> A numeric value associated with each edge

The igraph (*http://igraph.org/*) package has many powerful functions for manipulating and analyzing networks. One way to create an igraph object from tidy data is the graph_from_data_frame() function, which takes a data frame of edges with columns for "from," "to," and edge attributes (in this case n):

```
library(igraph)

# original counts
bigram_counts

## Source: local data frame [33,421 x 3]
## Groups: word1 [6,711]
##
##       word1     word2     n
##       <chr>     <chr> <int>
## 1       sir    thomas   287
## 2      miss  crawford   215
## 3   captain wentworth   170
## 4      miss woodhouse   162
## 5     frank churchill   132
## 6      lady   russell   118
## 7      lady   bertram   114
## 8       sir    walter   113
## 9      miss   fairfax   109
## 10   colonel   brandon   108
## # ... with 33,411 more rows

# filter for only relatively common combinations
bigram_graph <- bigram_counts %>%
  filter(n > 20) %>%
  graph_from_data_frame()

bigram_graph

## IGRAPH DN-- 91 77 --
## + attr: name (v/c), n (e/n)
## + edges (vertex names):
##  [1] sir       ->thomas     miss    ->crawford   captain ->wentworth
##  [4] miss      ->woodhouse  frank   ->churchill   lady    ->russell
##  [7] lady      ->bertram    sir     ->walter      miss    ->fairfax
## [10] colonel   ->brandon    miss    ->bates       lady    ->catherine
## [13] sir       ->john       jane    ->fairfax     miss    ->tilney
## [16] lady      ->middleton  miss    ->bingley     thousand->pounds
## [19] miss      ->dashwood   miss    ->bennet      john    ->knightley
```

```
## [22] miss    ->morland   captain ->benwick   dear    ->mis
## + ... omitted several edges
```

igraph has plotting functions built in, but they're not what the package is designed to do, so many other packages have developed visualization methods for graph objects. We recommend the ggraph package (Pedersen 2017), because it implements these visualizations in terms of the grammar of graphics, which we are already familiar with from ggplot2.

We can convert an igraph object into a ggraph with the ggraph function, after which we add layers to it, much like layers are added in ggplot2. For example, for a basic graph we need to add three layers: nodes, edges, and text (Figure 4-4).

```
library(ggraph)
set.seed(2017)

ggraph(bigram_graph, layout = "fr") +
  geom_edge_link() +
  geom_node_point() +
  geom_node_text(aes(label = name), vjust = 1, hjust = 1)
```

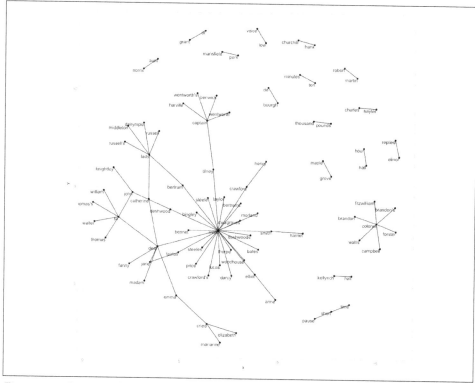

Figure 4-4. Common bigrams in Pride and Prejudice, showing those that occurred more than 20 times and where neither word was a stop word

In Figure 4-4, we can visualize some details of the text structure. For example, we see that salutations such as "miss," "lady," "sir," and "colonel" form common centers of nodes, which are often followed by names. We also see pairs or triplets along the outside that form common short phrases ("half hour," "thousand pounds," or "short time/pause").

We conclude with a few polishing operations to make a better-looking graph (Figure 4-5):

- We add the `edge_alpha` aesthetic to the link layer to make links transparent based on how common or rare the bigram is.
- We add directionality with an arrow, constructed using `grid::arrow()`, including an `end_cap` option that tells the arrow to end before touching the node.
- We tinker with the options to the node layer to make the nodes more attractive.
- We add a theme that's useful for plotting networks, `theme_void()`.

```
set.seed(2016)

a <- grid::arrow(type = "closed", length = unit(.15, "inches"))

ggraph(bigram_graph, layout = "fr") +
  geom_edge_link(aes(edge_alpha = n), show.legend = FALSE,
                 arrow = a, end_cap = circle(.07, 'inches')) +
  geom_node_point(color = "lightblue", size = 5) +
  geom_node_text(aes(label = name), vjust = 1, hjust = 1) +
  theme_void()
```

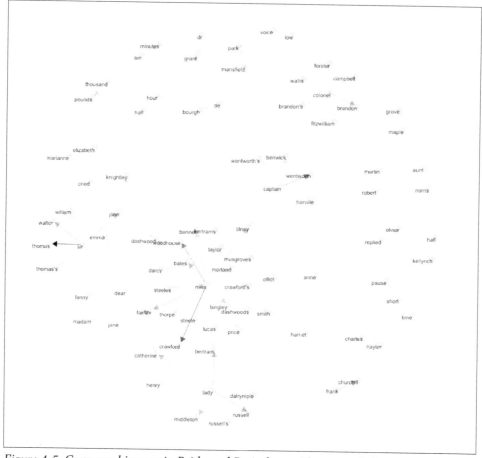

Figure 4-5. Common bigrams in Pride and Prejudice, with some polishing

It may take a some experimentation with ggraph to get your networks into a presentable format like this, but the network structure is a useful and flexible way to visualize relational tidy data.

Note that this is a visualization of a *Markov chain*, a common model in text processing. In a Markov chain, each choice of word depends only on the previous word. In this case, a random generator following this model might spit out "dear," then "sir," then "william/walter/thomas/thomas's" by following each word to the most common words that follow it. To make the visualization interpretable, we chose to show only the most common word-to-word connections, but one could imagine an enormous graph representing all connections that occur in the text.

Visualizing Bigrams in Other Texts

We went to a good amount of work in cleaning and visualizing bigrams on a text dataset, so let's collect it into a function so that we can easily perform it on other text datasets.

 To make it easy to use the functions `count_bigrams()` and `visualize_bigrams()` yourself, we've also reloaded the packages necessary for them.

```
library(dplyr)
library(tidyr)
library(tidytext)
library(ggplot2)
library(igraph)
library(ggraph)

count_bigrams <- function(dataset) {
  dataset %>%
    unnest_tokens(bigram, text, token = "ngrams", n = 2) %>%
    separate(bigram, c("word1", "word2"), sep = " ") %>%
    filter(!word1 %in% stop_words$word,
           !word2 %in% stop_words$word) %>%
    count(word1, word2, sort = TRUE)
}

visualize_bigrams <- function(bigrams) {
  set.seed(2016)
  a <- grid::arrow(type = "closed", length = unit(.15, "inches"))

  bigrams %>%
    graph_from_data_frame() %>%
    ggraph(layout = "fr") +
    geom_edge_link(aes(edge_alpha = n), show.legend = FALSE, arrow = a) +
    geom_node_point(color = "lightblue", size = 5) +
    geom_node_text(aes(label = name), vjust = 1, hjust = 1) +
    theme_void()
}
```

At this point, we could visualize bigrams in other works, such as the King James Bible (Figure 4-6):

```
# the King James version is book 10 on Project Gutenberg:
library(gutenbergr)
kjv <- gutenberg_download(10)

library(stringr)

kjv_bigrams <- kjv %>%
```

```
count_bigrams()

# filter out rare combinations, as well as digits
kjv_bigrams %>%
  filter(n > 40,
         !str_detect(word1, "\\d"),
         !str_detect(word2, "\\d")) %>%
  visualize_bigrams()
```

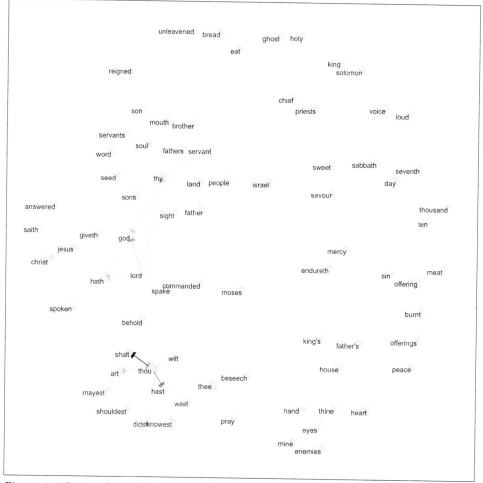

Figure 4-6. Directed graph of common bigrams in the King James Bible, showing those that occurred more than 40 times

Figure 4-6 thus lays out a common "blueprint" of language within the Bible, particularly focused around "thy" and "thou" (which could probably be considered stop words!). You can use the gutenbergr package and the count_bigrams/visual `ize_bigrams` functions to visualize bigrams in other classic books you're interested in.

Counting and Correlating Pairs of Words with the widyr Package

Tokenizing by n-gram is a useful way to explore pairs of adjacent words. However, we may also be interested in words that tend to co-occur within particular documents or particular chapters, even if they don't occur next to each other.

Tidy data is a useful structure for comparing between variables or grouping by rows, but it can be challenging to compare between rows: for example, to count the number of times that two words appear within the same document, or to see how correlated they are. Most operations for finding pairwise counts or correlations need to turn the data into a wide matrix first.

We'll examine some of the ways tidy text can be turned into a wide matrix in Chapter 5, but in this case it isn't necessary. The widyr (*https://github.com/dgrtwo/widyr*) package makes operations such as computing counts and correlations easy by simplifying the pattern of "widen data, perform an operation, then re-tidy data" (Figure 4-7). We'll focus on a set of functions that make pairwise comparisons between groups of observations (for example, between documents, or sections of text).

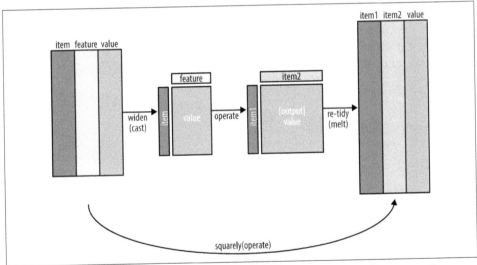

Figure 4-7. The philosophy behind the widyr package, which can perform operations such as counting and correlating on pairs of values in a tidy dataset. The widyr package first "casts" a tidy dataset into a wide matrix, performs an operation such as a correlation on it, then re-tidies the result.

Counting and Correlating Among Sections

Consider the book *Pride and Prejudice* divided into 10-line sections, as we did (with larger sections) for sentiment analysis in Chapter 2. We may be interested in what words tend to appear within the same section.

```
austen_section_words <- austen_books() %>%
  filter(book == "Pride & Prejudice") %>%
  mutate(section = row_number() %/% 10) %>%
  filter(section > 0) %>%
  unnest_tokens(word, text) %>%
  filter(!word %in% stop_words$word)

austen_section_words

## # A tibble: 37,240 × 3
##                  book section         word
##                 <fctr>   <dbl>        <chr>
## 1  Pride & Prejudice         1        truth
## 2  Pride & Prejudice         1  universally
## 3  Pride & Prejudice         1 acknowledged
## 4  Pride & Prejudice         1       single
## 5  Pride & Prejudice         1   possession
## 6  Pride & Prejudice         1      fortune
## 7  Pride & Prejudice         1         wife
## 8  Pride & Prejudice         1     feelings
## 9  Pride & Prejudice         1        views
## 10 Pride & Prejudice         1     entering
## # ... with 37,230 more rows
```

One useful function from widyr is the `pairwise_count()` function. The prefix `pairwise_` means it will result in one row for each pair of words in the `word` variable. This lets us count common pairs of words co-appearing within the same section.

```
library(widyr)

# count words co-occuring within sections
word_pairs <- austen_section_words %>%
  pairwise_count(word, section, sort = TRUE)

word_pairs

## # A tibble: 796,008 × 3
##       item1     item2     n
##       <chr>     <chr> <dbl>
## 1     darcy elizabeth   144
## 2 elizabeth     darcy   144
## 3      miss elizabeth   110
## 4 elizabeth      miss   110
## 5 elizabeth      jane   106
## 6      jane elizabeth   106
## 7      miss     darcy    92
## 8     darcy      miss    92
```

```
## 9   elizabeth   bingley    91
## 10    bingley elizabeth    91
## # ... with 795,998 more rows
```

Notice that while the input had one row for each pair of a document (a 10-line section) and a word, the output has one row for each pair of words. This is also a tidy format, but of a very different structure that we can use to answer new questions.

For example, we can see that the most common pair of words in a section is "Elizabeth" and "Darcy" (the two main characters). We can easily find the words that most often occur with Darcy.

```
word_pairs %>%
  filter(item1 == "darcy")

## # A tibble: 2,930 × 3
##      item1      item2      n
##      <chr>      <chr>  <dbl>
## 1   darcy elizabeth    144
## 2   darcy      miss     92
## 3   darcy   bingley     86
## 4   darcy      jane     46
## 5   darcy    bennet     45
## 6   darcy    sister     45
## 7   darcy      time     41
## 8   darcy      lady     38
## 9   darcy    friend     37
## 10  darcy   wickham     37
## # ... with 2,920 more rows
```

Examining Pairwise Correlation

Pairs like "Elizabeth" and "Darcy" are the most common co-occurring words, but that's not particularly meaningful since *they're also the most common individual words*. We may instead want to examine *correlation* among words, which indicates how often they appear together relative to how often they appear separately.

In particular, here we'll focus on the phi coefficient (*https://en.wikipedia.org/wiki/Phi_coefficient*), a common measure for binary correlation. The phi coefficient focuses on how much more likely it is that either *both* word X and Y appear, or *neither* do, than that one appears without the other.

Consider Table 4-1.

Table 4-1. Values used to calculate the phi coefficient

	Has word Y	No word Y	Total
Has word X	n_{11}	n_{10}	$n_{1.}$
No word X	n_{01}	n_{00}	$n_{0.}$
Total	$n_{.1}$	$n_{.0}$	n

For example, n_{11} represents the number of documents where both word X and word Y appear, n_{00} the number where neither appears, and n_{10} and n_{01} the cases where one appears without the other. In terms of this table, the phi coefficient is:

$$\phi = \frac{n_{11}n_{00} - n_{10}n_{01}}{\sqrt{n_{1.}\,n_{0.}\,n_{.0}\,n_{.1}}}$$

The phi coefficient is equivalent to the Pearson correlation, which you may have heard of elsewhere, when it is applied to binary data.

The `pairwise_cor()` function in widyr lets us find the phi coefficient between words based on how often they appear in the same section. Its syntax is similar to `pairwise_count()`.

```
# we need to filter for at least relatively common words first
word_cors <- austen_section_words %>%
  group_by(word) %>%
  filter(n() >= 20) %>%
  pairwise_cor(word, section, sort = TRUE)

word_cors

## # A tibble: 154,842 × 3
##         item1      item2 correlation
##         <chr>      <chr>       <dbl>
## 1      bourgh         de   0.9508501
## 2          de     bourgh   0.9508501
## 3      pounds   thousand   0.7005808
## 4    thousand     pounds   0.7005808
## 5     william        sir   0.6644719
## 6         sir    william   0.6644719
## 7    catherine      lady   0.6633048
## 8        lady  catherine   0.6633048
## 9      forster    colonel   0.6220950
## 10     colonel    forster   0.6220950
## # ... with 154,832 more rows
```

This output format is helpful for exploration. For example, we could find the words most correlated with a word like "pounds" using a `filter` operation.

```
word_cors %>%
  filter(item1 == "pounds")

## # A tibble: 393 × 3
##       item1      item2 correlation
##       <chr>      <chr>       <dbl>
## 1    pounds   thousand  0.70058081
```

```
## 2   pounds       ten  0.23057580
## 3   pounds   fortune  0.16386264
## 4   pounds   settled  0.14946049
## 5   pounds wickham's  0.14152401
## 6   pounds  children  0.12900011
## 7   pounds  mother's  0.11905928
## 8   pounds  believed  0.09321518
## 9   pounds    estate  0.08896876
## 10  pounds     ready  0.08597038
## # ... with 383 more rows
```

This lets us pick particular interesting words and find the other words most associated with them (Figure 4-8).

```
word_cors %>%
    filter(item1 %in% c("elizabeth", "pounds", "married", "pride")) %>%
    group_by(item1) %>%
    top_n(6) %>%
    ungroup() %>%
    mutate(item2 = reorder(item2, correlation)) %>%
    ggplot(aes(item2, correlation)) +
    geom_bar(stat = "identity") +
    facet_wrap(~ item1, scales = "free") +
    coord_flip()
```

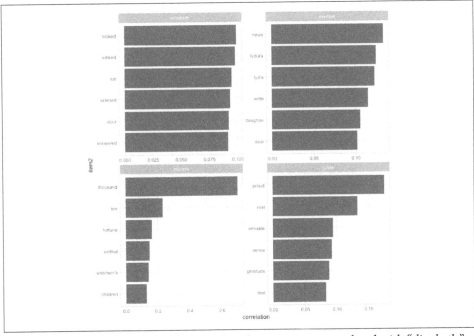

Figure 4-8. Words from Pride and Prejudice that were most correlated with "elizabeth," "pounds," "married," and "pride"

Just as we used ggraph to visualize bigrams, we can use it to visualize the correlations and clusters of words that were found by the widyr package (Figure 4-9).

```
set.seed(2016)

word_cors %>%
  filter(correlation > .15) %>%
  graph_from_data_frame() %>%
  ggraph(layout = "fr") +
  geom_edge_link(aes(edge_alpha = correlation), show.legend = FALSE) +
  geom_node_point(color = "lightblue", size = 5) +
  geom_node_text(aes(label = name), repel = TRUE) +
  theme_void()
```

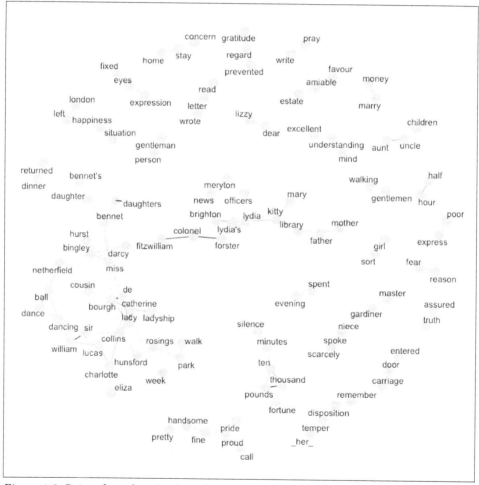

Figure 4-9. Pairs of words in Pride and Prejudice that show at least a 0.15 correlation of appearing within the same 10-line section

Note that unlike the bigram analysis, the relationships here are symmetrical, rather than directional (there are no arrows). We can also see that while pairings of names and titles that dominated bigram pairings are common, such as "colonel/fitzwilliam," we can also see pairings of words that appear close to each other, such as "walk" and "park," or "dance" and "ball."

Summary

This chapter showed how the tidy text approach is useful not only for analyzing individual words, but also for exploring the relationships and connections between words. Such relationships can involve n-grams, which enable us to see what words tend to appear after others, or co-occurences and correlations, for words that appear in proximity to each other. This chapter also demonstrated the ggraph package for visualizing both of these types of relationships as networks. These network visualizations are a flexible tool for exploring relationships, and will play an important role in the case studies in later chapters.

## CHAPTER 5

Converting to and from Nontidy Formats

In the previous chapters, we've been analyzing text arranged in the tidy text format: a table with one token per document per row, such as is constructed by the function unnest_tokens(). This lets us use the popular suite of tidy tools such as dplyr, tidyr, and ggplot2 to explore and visualize text data. We've demonstrated that many informative text analyses can be performed using these tools.

However, most of the existing R tools for natural language processing, besides the tidytext package, aren't compatible with this format. The CRAN Task View for Natural Language Processing (*https://cran.r-project.org/web/views/NaturalLanguageProcessing.html*) lists a large selection of packages that take other structures of input and provide nontidy outputs. These packages are very useful in text mining applications, and many existing text datasets are structured according to these formats.

Computer scientist Hal Abelson has observed that, "No matter how complex and polished the individual operations are, it is often the quality of the glue that most directly determines the power of the system" (Abelson 2008). In that spirit, this chapter will discuss the "glue" that connects the tidy text format with other important packages and data structures, allowing you to rely on both existing text mining packages and the suite of tidy tools to perform your analysis.

Figure 5-1 illustrates how an analysis might switch between tidy and nontidy data structures and tools. This chapter will focus on the process of tidying document-term matrices, as well as casting a tidy data frame into a sparse matrix. We'll also explore how to tidy Corpus objects, which combine raw text with document metadata, into text data frames, leading to a case study of ingesting and analyzing financial articles.

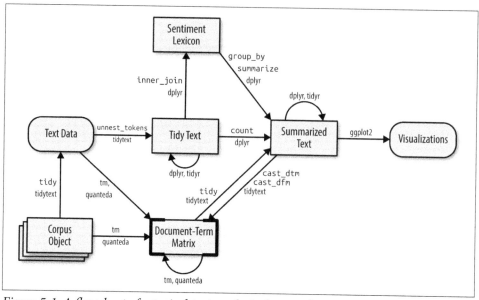

Figure 5-1. A flowchart of a typical text analysis that combines tidytext with other tools and data formats, particularly the tm or quanteda packages. This chapter shows how to convert back and forth between document-term matrices and tidy data frames, as well as convert from a Corpus object to a text data frame.

Tidying a Document-Term Matrix

One of the most common structures that text mining packages work with is the document-term matrix (*https://en.wikipedia.org/wiki/Document-term_matrix*) (or DTM). This is a matrix where:

- Each row represents one document (such as a book or article).
- Each column represents one term.
- Each value (typically) contains the number of appearances of that term in that document.

Since most pairings of document and term do not occur (they have the value zero), DTMs are usually implemented as sparse matrices. These objects can be treated as though they were matrices (for example, accessing particular rows and columns), but are stored in a more efficient format. We'll discuss several implementations of these matrices in this chapter.

DTM objects cannot be used directly with tidy tools, just as tidy data frames cannot be used as input for most text mining packages. Thus, the tidytext package provides two verbs that convert between the two formats:

- `tidy()` turns a document-term matrix into a tidy data frame. This verb comes from the broom package (Robinson 2017), which provides similar tidying functions for many statistical models and objects.

- `cast()` turns a tidy one-term-per-row data frame into a matrix. tidytext provides three variations of this verb, each converting to a different type of matrix: `cast_sparse()` (converting to a sparse matrix from the Matrix package), `cast_dtm()` (converting to a `DocumentTermMatrix` object from tm), and `cast_dfm()` (converting to a `dfm` object from quanteda).

As shown in Figure 5-1, a DTM is typically comparable to a tidy data frame after a count or a `group_by`/`summarize` that contains counts or another statistic for each combination of a term and document.

Tidying DocumentTermMatrix Objects

Perhaps the most widely used implementation of DTMs in R is the `DocumentTermMatrix` class in the tm package. Many available text mining datasets are provided in this format. For example, consider the collection of Associated Press newspaper articles included in the topicmodels package.

```
library(tm)

data("AssociatedPress", package = "topicmodels")
AssociatedPress

## <<DocumentTermMatrix (documents: 2246, terms: 10473)>>
## Non-/sparse entries: 302031/23220327
## Sparsity           : 99%
## Maximal term length: 18
## Weighting          : term frequency (tf)
```

We see that this dataset contains documents (each of them an AP article) and terms (distinct words). Notice that this DTM is 99% sparse (99% of document-word pairs are zero). We could access the terms in the document with the `Terms()` function.

```
terms <- Terms(AssociatedPress)
head(terms)

## [1] "aaron"     "abandon"     "abandoned"  "abandoning" "abbott"     "abboud"
```

If we wanted to analyze this data with tidy tools, we would first need to turn it into a data frame with one token per document per row. The broom package introduced the `tidy()` verb, which takes a nontidy object and turns it into a tidy data frame. The tidytext package implements this method for `DocumentTermMatrix` objects.

```
library(dplyr)
library(tidytext)

ap_td <- tidy(AssociatedPress)
ap_td

## # A tibble: 302,031 × 3
##     document       term count
##        <int>      <chr> <dbl>
## 1          1     adding     1
## 2          1      adult     2
## 3          1        ago     1
## 4          1    alcohol     1
## 5          1  allegedly     1
## 6          1      allen     1
## 7          1 apparently     2
## 8          1   appeared     1
## 9          1   arrested     1
## 10         1    assault     1
## # ... with 302,021 more rows
```

Notice that we now have a tidy three-column `tbl_df`, with variables `document`, `term`, and `count`. This tidying operation is similar to the `melt()` function from the reshape2 package (Wickham 2007) for nonsparse matrices.

 Notice that only the nonzero values are included in the tidied output: document 1 includes terms such as "adding" and "adult," but not "aaron" or "abandon." This means the tidied version has no rows where `count` is zero.

As we've seen in previous chapters, this form is convenient for analysis with the dplyr, tidytext, and ggplot2 packages. For example, you can perform sentiment analysis on these newspaper articles with the approach described in Chapter 2.

```
ap_sentiments <- ap_td %>%
  inner_join(get_sentiments("bing"), by = c(term = "word"))

ap_sentiments

## # A tibble: 30,094 × 4
##     document     term count sentiment
##        <int>    <chr> <dbl>     <chr>
## 1          1   assault     1  negative
## 2          1   complex     1  negative
## 3          1     death     1  negative
## 4          1      died     1  negative
## 5          1      good     2  positive
## 6          1   illness     1  negative
## 7          1    killed     2  negative
## 8          1      like     2  positive
## 9          1     liked     1  positive
```

```
## 10        1 miracle     1 positive
## # ... with 30,084 more rows
```

This would let us visualize which words from the AP articles most often contributed to positive or negative sentiment, seen in Figure 5-2. We can see that the most common positive words include "like," "work," "support," and "good," while the most negative words include "killed," "death," and "vice." (The inclusion of "vice" as a negative term is probably a mistake on the algorithm's part, since it likely usually refers to "vice president").

```
library(ggplot2)

ap_sentiments %>%
  count(sentiment, term, wt = count) %>%
  ungroup() %>%
  filter(n >= 200) %>%
  mutate(n = ifelse(sentiment == "negative", -n, n)) %>%
  mutate(term = reorder(term, n)) %>%
  ggplot(aes(term, n, fill = sentiment)) +
  geom_bar(stat = "identity") +
  ylab("Contribution to sentiment") +
  coord_flip()
```

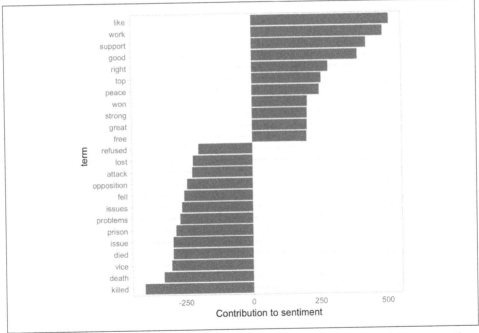

Figure 5-2. Words from AP articles with the greatest contribution to positive or negative sentiments, computed as the product of the word's AFINN sentiment score and its frequency.

Tidying dfm Objects

Other text mining packages provide alternative implementations of document-term matrices, such as the dfm (document-feature matrix) class from the quanteda package (Benoit and Nulty 2016). For example, the quanteda package comes with a corpus of presidential inauguration speeches, which can be converted to a dfm using the appropriate function.

```
library(methods)

data("data_corpus_inaugural", package = "quanteda")
inaug_dfm <- quanteda::dfm(data_corpus_inaugural, verbose = FALSE)

inaug_dfm

## Document-feature matrix of: 58 documents, 9,232 features (91.6% sparse).
```

The tidy method works on these document-feature matrices as well, turning them into a one-token-per-document-per-row table.

```
inaug_td <- tidy(inaug_dfm)
inaug_td

## # A tibble: 44,725 × 3
##             document    term count
##                <chr>   <chr> <dbl>
## 1   1789-Washington  fellow     3
## 2   1793-Washington  fellow     1
## 3        1797-Adams  fellow     3
## 4    1801-Jefferson  fellow     7
## 5    1805-Jefferson  fellow     8
## 6     1809-Madison  fellow     1
## 7     1813-Madison  fellow     1
## 8      1817-Monroe  fellow     6
## 9      1821-Monroe  fellow    10
## 10      1825-Adams  fellow     3
## # ... with 44,715 more rows
```

We may be interested in finding the words most specific to each of the inaugural speeches. This could be quantified by calculating the tf-idf of each term-speech pair using the bind_tf_idf() function, as described in Chapter 3.

```
inaug_tf_idf <- inaug_td %>%
  bind_tf_idf(term, document, count) %>%
  arrange(desc(tf_idf))

inaug_tf_idf

## # A tibble: 44,725 × 6
##             document        term count          tf      idf    tf_idf
##                <chr>       <chr> <dbl>       <dbl>    <dbl>     <dbl>
## 1   1793-Washington      arrive     1 0.006802721 4.060443 0.02762206
## 2   1793-Washington  upbraidings     1 0.006802721 4.060443 0.02762206
```

```
## 3   1793-Washington     violated   1 0.006802721 3.367296 0.02290677
## 4   1793-Washington     willingly  1 0.006802721 3.367296 0.02290677
## 5   1793-Washington     incurring  1 0.006802721 3.367296 0.02290677
## 6   1793-Washington     previous   1 0.006802721 2.961831 0.02014851
## 7   1793-Washington     knowingly  1 0.006802721 2.961831 0.02014851
## 8   1793-Washington    injunctions 1 0.006802721 2.961831 0.02014851
## 9   1793-Washington     witnesses  1 0.006802721 2.961831 0.02014851
## 10  1793-Washington     besides    1 0.006802721 2.674149 0.01819149
## # ... with 44,715 more rows
```

We could use this data to pick four notable inaugural addresses (from Presidents Lincoln, Roosevelt, Kennedy, and Obama), and visualize the words most specific to each speech, as shown in Figure 5-3.

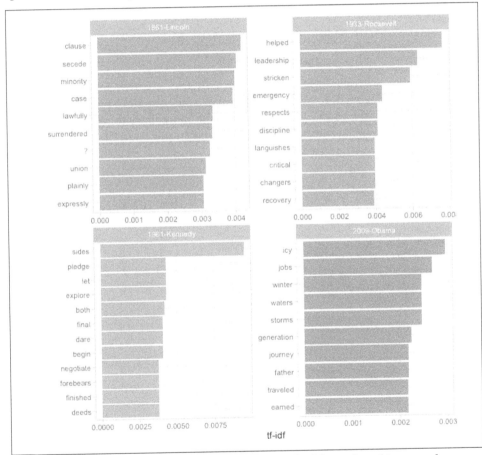

Figure 5-3. The terms with the highest tf-idf from each of four selected inaugural addresses. Note that quanteda's tokenizer includes the "?" punctuation mark as a term, though the texts we've tokenized ourselves with unnest_tokens do not.

As another example of a visualization possible with tidy data, we could extract the year from each document's name, and compute the total number of words within each year.

 Note that we've used tidyr's `complete()` function to include zeroes (cases where a word doesn't appear in a document) in the table.

```
library(tidyr)

year_term_counts <- inaug_td %>%
  extract(document, "year", "(\\d+)", convert = TRUE) %>%
  complete(year, term, fill = list(count = 0)) %>%
  group_by(year) %>%
  mutate(year_total = sum(count))
```

This lets us pick several words and visualize how they changed in frequency over time, as shown in Figure 5-4. We can see that over time, American presidents became less likely to refer to the country as the "Union" and more likely to refer to "America." They also became less likely to talk about the "Constitution" and "foreign" countries, and more likely to mention "freedom" and "God."

```
year_term_counts %>%
  filter(term %in% c("god", "america", "foreign",
                     "union", "constitution", "freedom")) %>%
  ggplot(aes(year, count / year_total)) +
  geom_point() +
  geom_smooth() +
  facet_wrap(~ term, scales = "free_y") +
  scale_y_continuous(labels = scales::percent_format()) +
  ylab("% frequency of word in inaugural address")
```

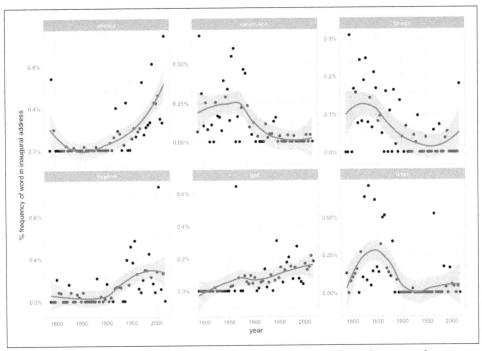

Figure 5-4. Changes in word frequency over time within Presidential inaugural addresses, for four selected terms

These examples show how you can use tidytext, and the related suite of tidy tools, to analyze sources even if their origin is not in a tidy format.

Casting Tidy Text Data into a Matrix

Just as some existing text mining packages provide document-term matrices as sample data or output, some algorithms expect such matrices as input. Therefore, tidytext provides `cast_` verbs for converting from a tidy form to these matrices.

For example, we could take the tidied AP dataset and cast it back into a document-term matrix using the `cast_dtm()` function.

```
ap_td %>%
  cast_dtm(document, term, count)

## <<DocumentTermMatrix (documents: 2246, terms: 10473)>>
## Non-/sparse entries: 302031/23220327
## Sparsity           : 99%
## Maximal term length: 18
## Weighting          : term frequency (tf)
```

Similarly, we could cast the table into a `dfm` object from quanteda's dfm with `cast_dfm()`.

```
ap_td %>%
  cast_dfm(term, document, count)

## Document-feature matrix of: 10,473 documents, 2,246 features (98.7% sparse).
```

Some tools simply require a sparse matrix.

```
library(Matrix)

# cast into a Matrix object
m <- ap_td %>%
  cast_sparse(document, term, count)

class(m)

## [1] "dgCMatrix"
## attr(,"package")
## [1] "Matrix"

dim(m)

## [1]  2246 10473
```

This kind of conversion could easily be done from any of the tidy text structures we've used so far in this book. For example, we could create a DTM of Jane Austen's books in just a few lines of code.

```
library(janeaustenr)

austen_dtm <- austen_books() %>%
  unnest_tokens(word, text) %>%
  count(book, word) %>%
  cast_dtm(book, word, n)

austen_dtm

## <<DocumentTermMatrix (documents: 6, terms: 14520)>>
## Non-/sparse entries: 40379/46741
## Sparsity           : 54%
## Maximal term length: 19
## Weighting          : term frequency (tf)
```

This casting process allows for reading, filtering, and processing to be done using dplyr and other tidy tools, after which the data can be converted into a document-term matrix for machine learning applications. In Chapter 6, we'll examine some examples where a tidy text dataset has to be converted into a `DocumentTermMatrix` for processing.

Tidying Corpus Objects with Metadata

Some data structures are designed to store document collections *before* tokenization, often called a "corpus." One common example is Corpus objects from the tm package. These store text alongside *metadata*, which may include an ID, date/time, title, or language for each document.

For example, the tm package comes with the acq corpus, containing 50 articles from the news service Reuters.

```
data("acq")
acq

## <<VCorpus>>
## Metadata:  corpus specific: 0, document level (indexed): 0
## Content:  documents: 50

# first document
acq[[1]]

## <<PlainTextDocument>>
## Metadata:  15
## Content:  chars: 1287
```

A Corpus object is structured like a list, with each item containing both text and metadata (see the tm documentation for more on working with Corpus objects). This is a flexible storage method for documents, but doesn't lend itself to processing with tidy tools.

We can thus use the tidy() method to construct a table with one row per document, including the metadata (such as id and datetimestamp) as columns alongside the text.

```
acq_td <- tidy(acq)
acq_td

## # A tibble: 50 × 16
##                           author        datetimestamp description
##                            <chr>                <dttm>       <chr>
## 1                           <NA> 1987-02-26 10:18:06
## 2                           <NA> 1987-02-26 10:19:15
## 3                           <NA> 1987-02-26 10:49:56
## 4   By Cal Mankowski, Reuters 1987-02-26 10:51:17
## 5                           <NA> 1987-02-26 11:08:33
## 6                           <NA> 1987-02-26 11:32:37
## 7      By Patti Domm, Reuter 1987-02-26 11:43:13
## 8                           <NA> 1987-02-26 11:59:25
## 9                           <NA> 1987-02-26 12:01:28
## 10                          <NA> 1987-02-26 12:08:27
##                                          heading    id language
##                                           <chr> <chr>    <chr>
## 1    COMPUTER TERMINAL SYSTEMS <CPML> COMPLETES SALE    10       en
```

```
## 2       OHIO MATTRESS <OMT> MAY HAVE LOWER 1ST QTR NET    12    en
## 3         MCLEAN'S <MII> U.S. LINES SETS ASSET TRANSFER    44    en
## 4      CHEMLAWN <CHEM> RISES ON HOPES FOR HIGHER BIDS      45    en
## 5      <COFAB INC> BUYS GULFEX FOR UNDISCLOSED AMOUNT      68    en
## 6          INVESTMENT FIRMS CUT CYCLOPS <CYL> STAKE        96    en
## 7    AMERICAN EXPRESS <AXP> SEEN IN POSSIBLE SPINNOFF     110    en
## 8     HONG KONG FIRM UPS WRATHER<WCO> STAKE TO 11 PCT     125    en
## 9                LIEBERT CORP <LIEB> APPROVES MERGER      128    en
## 10      GULF APPLIED TECHNOLOGIES <GATS> SELLS UNITS      134    en
## # ... with 40 more rows, and 10 more variables: language <chr>, origin <chr>,
## #   topics <chr>, lewissplit <chr>, cgisplit <chr>, oldid <chr>,
## #   places <list>, people <lgl>, orgs <lgl>, exchanges <lgl>, text <chr>
```

This can then be used with `unnest_tokens()` to, for example, find the most common words across the 50 Reuters articles, or the ones most specific to each article.

```
acq_tokens <- acq_td %>%
  select(-places) %>%
  unnest_tokens(word, text) %>%
  anti_join(stop_words, by = "word")

# most common words
acq_tokens %>%
  count(word, sort = TRUE)

## # A tibble: 1,566 × 2
##        word     n
##       <chr> <int>
## 1      dlrs   100
## 2       pct    70
## 3       mln    65
## 4   company    63
## 5    shares    52
## 6    reuter    50
## 7     stock    46
## 8     offer    34
## 9     share    34
## 10 american    28
## # ... with 1,556 more rows

# tf-idf
acq_tokens %>%
  count(id, word) %>%
  bind_tf_idf(word, id, n) %>%
  arrange(desc(tf_idf))

## Source: local data frame [2,853 x 6]
## Groups: id [50]
##
##        id    word     n        tf      idf    tf_idf
##     <chr>   <chr> <int>     <dbl>    <dbl>     <dbl>
## 1     186  groupe     2 0.13333333 3.912023 0.5216031
## 2     128 liebert     3 0.13043478 3.912023 0.5102639
## 3     474 esselte     5 0.10869565 3.912023 0.4252199
```

```
## 4     371  burdett    6 0.10344828 3.912023 0.4046920
## 5     442 hazleton    4 0.10256410 3.912023 0.4012331
## 6     199  circuit    5 0.10204082 3.912023 0.3991860
## 7     162 suffield    2 0.10000000 3.912023 0.3912023
## 8     498     west    3 0.10000000 3.912023 0.3912023
## 9     441      rmj    8 0.12121212 3.218876 0.3901668
## 10    467  nursery    3 0.09677419 3.912023 0.3785829
## # ... with 2,843 more rows
```

Example: Mining Financial Articles

Corpus objects are a common output format for data-ingesting packages, which means the `tidy()` function gives us access to a wide variety of text data. One example is tm.plugin.webmining (*https://cran.r-project.org/package=tm.plugin.webmining*), which connects to online feeds to retrieve news articles based on a keyword. For instance, performing `WebCorpus(GoogleFinanceSource("NASDAQ:MSFT")))` allows us to retrieve the 20 most recent articles related to the Microsoft (MSFT) stock.

Here we'll retrieve recent articles relevant to nine major technology stocks: Microsoft, Apple, Google, Amazon, Facebook, Twitter, IBM, Yahoo, and Netflix.

These results were downloaded in January 2017, when this chapter was written, so you'll certainly find different results if you run it for yourself. Note that this code takes several minutes to run.

```
library(tm.plugin.webmining)
library(purrr)

company <- c("Microsoft", "Apple", "Google", "Amazon", "Facebook",
             "Twitter", "IBM", "Yahoo", "Netflix")
symbol <- c("MSFT", "AAPL", "GOOG", "AMZN", "FB", "TWTR", "IBM", "YHOO", "NFLX")

download_articles <- function(symbol) {
  WebCorpus(GoogleFinanceSource(paste0("NASDAQ:", symbol)))
}

stock_articles <- data_frame(company = company,
                             symbol = symbol) %>%
  mutate(corpus = map(symbol, download_articles))
```

This uses the `map()` function from the purrr package, which applies a function to each item in `symbol` to create a list, which we store in the corpus list column.

```
stock_articles
```

```
## # A tibble: 9 × 3
##      company symbol       corpus
##        <chr>  <chr>       <list>
```

```
## 1 Microsoft    MSFT <S3: WebCorpus>
## 2    Apple     AAPL <S3: WebCorpus>
## 3   Google     GOOG <S3: WebCorpus>
## 4   Amazon     AMZN <S3: WebCorpus>
## 5 Facebook       FB <S3: WebCorpus>
## 6  Twitter     TWTR <S3: WebCorpus>
## 7      IBM      IBM <S3: WebCorpus>
## 8    Yahoo     YHOO <S3: WebCorpus>
## 9  Netflix     NFLX <S3: WebCorpus>
```

Each of the items in the `corpus` list column is a `WebCorpus` object, which is a special case of a corpus like `acq`. We can thus turn each into a data frame using the `tidy()` function, unnest it with tidyr's `unnest()`, then tokenize the `text` column of the individual articles using `unnest_tokens()`.

```
stock_tokens <- stock_articles %>%
  unnest(map(corpus, tidy)) %>%
  unnest_tokens(word, text) %>%
  select(company, datetimestamp, word, id, heading)

stock_tokens
```

```
## # A tibble: 105,057 × 5
##       company       datetimestamp        word
##         <chr>               <dttm>       <chr>
## 1  Microsoft 2017-01-17 07:07:24   microsoft
## 2  Microsoft 2017-01-17 07:07:24 corporation
## 3  Microsoft 2017-01-17 07:07:24        data
## 4  Microsoft 2017-01-17 07:07:24     privacy
## 5  Microsoft 2017-01-17 07:07:24       could
## 6  Microsoft 2017-01-17 07:07:24        send
## 7  Microsoft 2017-01-17 07:07:24        msft
## 8  Microsoft 2017-01-17 07:07:24       stock
## 9  Microsoft 2017-01-17 07:07:24     soaring
## 10 Microsoft 2017-01-17 07:07:24          by
## # ... with 105,047 more rows, and 2 more variables: id <chr>, heading <chr>
```

Here we see some of each article's metadata alongside the words used. We could use tf-idf to determine which words were most specific to each stock symbol.

```
library(stringr)

stock_tf_idf <- stock_tokens %>%
  count(company, word) %>%
  filter(!str_detect(word, "\\d+")) %>%
  bind_tf_idf(word, company, n) %>%
  arrange(-tf_idf)
```

The top terms for each are visualized in Figure 5-5. As we'd expect, the company's name and symbol are typically included, but so are several of their product offerings and executives, as well as companies they are making deals with (such as Disney with Netflix).

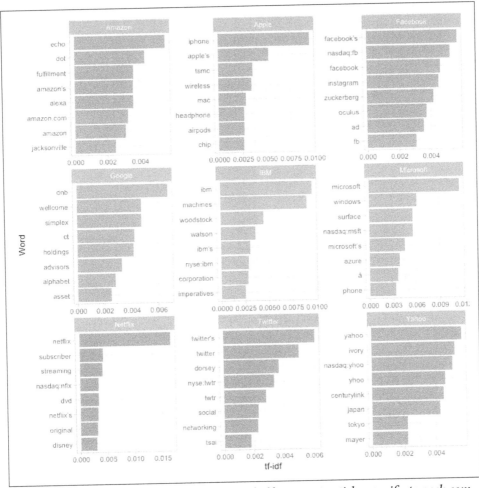

Figure 5-5. The eight words with the highest tf-idf in recent articles specific to each company

If we were interested in using recent news to analyze the market and make investment decisions, we'd likely want to use sentiment analysis to determine whether the news coverage was positive or negative. Before we run such an analysis, we should look at what words would contribute the most to positive and negative sentiments, as was shown in "Most Common Positive and Negative Words" on page 22. For example, we could examine this within the AFINN lexicon (Figure 5-6).

```
stock_tokens %>%
  anti_join(stop_words, by = "word") %>%
  count(word, id, sort = TRUE) %>%
  inner_join(get_sentiments("afinn"), by = "word") %>%
  group_by(word) %>%
```

```
summarize(contribution = sum(n * score)) %>%
top_n(12, abs(contribution)) %>%
mutate(word = reorder(word, contribution)) %>%
ggplot(aes(word, contribution)) +
geom_col() +
coord_flip() +
labs(y = "Frequency of word * AFINN score")
```

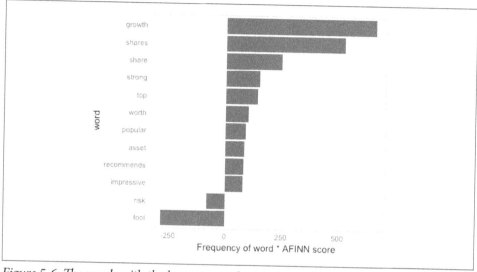

Figure 5-6. The words with the largest contribution to sentiment scores in recent financial articles, according to the AFINN dictionary. The "contribution" is the product of the word and the sentiment score.

In the context of these financial articles, there are a few big red flags here. The words "share" and "shares" are counted as positive verbs by the AFINN lexicon ("Alice will **share** her cake with Bob"), but they're actually neutral nouns ("The stock price is $12 per **share**") that could just as easily be in a positive sentence as a negative one. The word "fool" is even more deceptive: it refers to Motley Fool, a financial services company. In short, we can see that the AFINN sentiment lexicon is entirely unsuited to the context of financial data (as are the NRC and Bing lexicons).

Instead, we introduce another sentiment lexicon: the Loughran and McDonald dictionary of financial sentiment terms (Loughran and McDonald 2011). This dictionary was developed based on analyses of financial reports, and intentionally avoids words like "share" and "fool," as well as subtler terms like "liability" and "risk" that may not have a negative meaning in a financial context.

The Loughran data divides words into six sentiments: "positive," "negative," "litigious," "uncertain," "constraining," and "superfluous." We could start by examining

the most common words belonging to each sentiment within this text dataset
(Figure 5-7).

```
stock_tokens %>%
  count(word) %>%
  inner_join(get_sentiments("loughran"), by = "word") %>%
  group_by(sentiment) %>%
  top_n(5, n) %>%
  ungroup() %>%
  mutate(word = reorder(word, n)) %>%
  ggplot(aes(word, n)) +
  geom_col() +
  coord_flip() +
  facet_wrap(~ sentiment, scales = "free") +
  ylab("Frequency of this word in the recent financial articles")
```

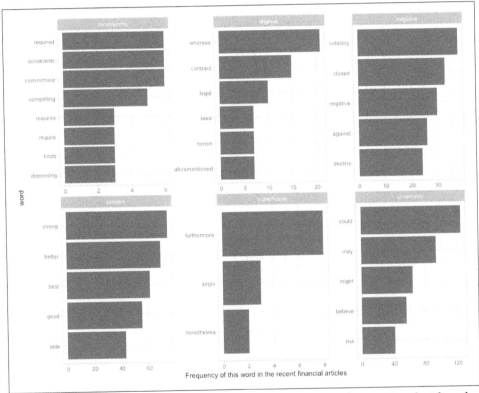

Figure 5-7. The most common words in the financial news articles associated with each of the six sentiments in the Loughran and McDonald lexicon

These assignments (Figure 5-7) of words to sentiments look more reasonable: common positive words include "strong" and "better," but not "shares" or "growth," while negative words include "volatility" but not "fool." The other sentiments look reasonable as well: the most common "uncertainty" terms include "could" and "may."

Now that we know we can trust the dictionary to approximate the articles' sentiments, we can use our typical methods for counting the number of uses of each sentiment-associated word in each corpus.

```
stock_sentiment_count <- stock_tokens %>%
  inner_join(get_sentiments("loughran"), by = "word") %>%
  count(sentiment, company) %>%
  spread(sentiment, n, fill = 0)

stock_sentiment_count
```

```
## # A tibble: 9 x 7
##      company constraining litigious negative positive superfluous uncertainty
## *      <chr>        <dbl>     <dbl>    <dbl>    <dbl>       <dbl>       <dbl>
## 1      Amazon           7         8       84      144           3          70
## 2       Apple           9        11      161      156           2         132
## 3    Facebook           4        32      128      150           4          81
## 4      Google           7         8       60      103           0          58
## 5         IBM           8        22      147      148           0         104
## 6   Microsoft           6        19       92      129           3         116
## 7     Netflix           4         7      111      162           0         106
## 8     Twitter           4        12      157       79           1          75
## 9       Yahoo           3        28      130       74           0          71
```

It might be interesting to examine which company has the most news with "litigious" or "uncertain" terms. But the simplest measure, much as it was for most analyses in Chapter 2, is to see whether the news is more positive or negative. As a general quantitative measure of sentiment, we'll use (positive - negative) / (positive + negative) (Figure 5-8).

```
stock_sentiment_count %>%
  mutate(score = (positive - negative) / (positive + negative)) %>%
  mutate(company = reorder(company, score)) %>%
  ggplot(aes(company, score, fill = score > 0)) +
  geom_col(show.legend = FALSE) +
  coord_flip() +
  labs(x = "Company",
       y = "Positivity score among 20 recent news articles")
```

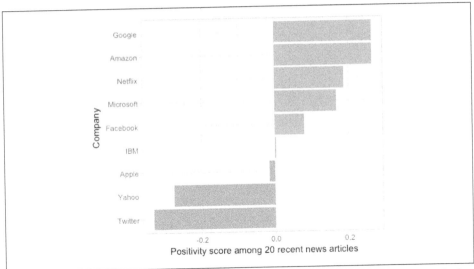

Figure 5-8. "Positivity" of the news coverage around each stock in January 2017, calculated as (positive - negative) / (positive + negative), based on uses of positive and negative words in 20 recent news articles about each company

Based on this analysis, we'd say that in January 2017, most of the coverage of Yahoo and Twitter was strongly negative, while coverage of Google and Amazon was the most positive. A glance at current financial headlines suggests that it's on the right track. If you were interested in further analysis, you could use one of R's many quantitative finance packages to compare these articles to recent stock prices and other metrics.

Summary

Text analysis requires working with a variety of tools, many of which have inputs and outputs that aren't in a tidy form. This chapter showed how to convert between a tidy text data frame and sparse document-term matrices, as well as how to tidy a Corpus object containing document metadata. The next chapter will demonstrate another notable example of a package, topicmodels, that requires a document-term matrix as input, showing that these conversion tools are an essential part of text analysis.

## CHAPTER 6

Topic Modeling

In text mining, we often have collections of documents, such as blog posts or news articles, that we'd like to divide into natural groups so that we can understand them separately. Topic modeling is a method for unsupervised classification of such documents, similar to clustering on numeric data, which finds natural groups of items even when we're not sure what we're looking for.

Latent Dirichlet allocation (LDA) is a particularly popular method for fitting a topic model. It treats each document as a mixture of topics, and each topic as a mixture of words. This allows documents to "overlap" each other in terms of content, rather than being separated into discrete groups, in a way that mirrors typical use of natural language.

As Figure 6-1 shows, we can use tidy text principles to approach topic modeling with the same set of tidy tools we've used throughout this book. In this chapter, we'll learn to work with LDA objects from the topicmodels package (*https://cran.r-project.org/ package=topicmodels*), particularly tidying such models so that they can be manipulated with ggplot2 and dplyr. We'll also explore an example of clustering chapters from several books, where we can see that a topic model "learns" to tell the difference between the four books based on the text content.

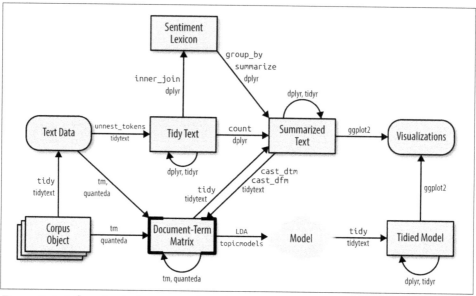

Figure 6-1. A flowchart of a text analysis that incorporates topic modeling. The topicmodels package takes a document-term matrix as input and produces a model that can be tidied by tidytext, such that it can be manipulated and visualized with dplyr and ggplot2.

Latent Dirichlet Allocation

Latent Dirichlet allocation is one of the most common algorithms for topic modeling. Without diving into the math behind the model, we can understand it as being guided by two principles:

Every document is a mixture of topics
> We imagine that each document may contain words from several topics in particular proportions. For example, in a two-topic model we could say "Document 1 is 90% topic A and 10% topic B, while Document 2 is 30% topic A and 70% topic B."

Every topic is a mixture of words
> For example, we could imagine a two-topic model of American news, with one topic for "politics" and one for "entertainment." The most common words in the politics topic might be "President," "Congress," and "government," while the entertainment topic may be made up of words such as "movies," "television," and "actor." Importantly, words can be shared between topics; a word like "budget" might appear in both equally.

LDA is a mathematical method for estimating both of these at the same time: finding the mixture of words that is associated with each topic, while also determining the mixture of topics that describes each document. There are a number of existing implementations of this algorithm, and we'll explore one of them in depth.

In Chapter 5 we briefly introduced the `AssociatedPress` dataset, provided by the topicmodels package, as an example of a `DocumentTermMatrix`. This is a collection of 2,246 news articles from an American news agency, mostly published around 1988.

```
library(topicmodels)

data("AssociatedPress")
AssociatedPress

## <<DocumentTermMatrix (documents: 2246, terms: 10473)>>
## Non-/sparse entries: 302031/23220327
## Sparsity           : 99%
## Maximal term length: 18
## Weighting          : term frequency (tf)
```

We can use the `LDA()` function from the topicmodels package, setting k = 2, to create a two-topic LDA model.

Almost any topic model in practice will use a larger k, but we will soon see that this analysis approach extends to a larger number of topics.

This function returns an object containing the full details of the model fit, such as how words are associated with topics and how topics are associated with documents.

```
# set a seed so that the output of the model is predictable
ap_lda <- LDA(AssociatedPress, k = 2, control = list(seed = 1234))
ap_lda

## A LDA_VEM topic model with 2 topics.
```

Fitting the model was the "easy part": the rest of the analysis will involve exploring and interpreting the model using tidying functions from the tidytext package.

Word-Topic Probabilities

In Chapter 5 we introduced the `tidy()` method, originally from the broom package (Robinson 2017), for tidying model objects. The tidytext package provides this method for extracting the per-topic-per-word probabilities, called β ("beta"), from the model.

```
library(tidytext)

ap_topics <- tidy(ap_lda, matrix = "beta")
ap_topics

## # A tibble: 20,946 × 3
##    topic       term         beta
##    <int>      <chr>        <dbl>
## 1      1      aaron 1.686917e-12
## 2      2      aaron 3.895941e-05
## 3      1    abandon 2.654910e-05
## 4      2    abandon 3.990786e-05
## 5      1  abandoned 1.390663e-04
## 6      2  abandoned 5.876946e-05
## 7      1 abandoning 2.454843e-33
## 8      2 abandoning 2.337565e-05
## 9      1     abbott 2.130484e-06
## 10     2     abbott 2.968045e-05
## # ... with 20,936 more rows
```

Notice that this has turned the model into a one-topic-per-term-per-row format. For each combination, the model computes the probability of that term being generated from that topic. For example, the term "aaron" has a 1.686917×10^{-12} probability of being generated from topic 1, but a 3.8959408×10^{-5} probability of being generated from topic 2.

We could use dplyr's top_n() to find the 10 terms that are most common within each topic. As a tidy data frame, this lends itself well to a ggplot2 visualization (Figure 6-2).

```
library(ggplot2)
library(dplyr)

ap_top_terms <- ap_topics %>%
  group_by(topic) %>%
  top_n(10, beta) %>%
  ungroup() %>%
  arrange(topic, -beta)

ap_top_terms %>%
  mutate(term = reorder(term, beta)) %>%
  ggplot(aes(term, beta, fill = factor(topic))) +
  geom_col(show.legend = FALSE) +
  facet_wrap(~ topic, scales = "free") +
  coord_flip()
```

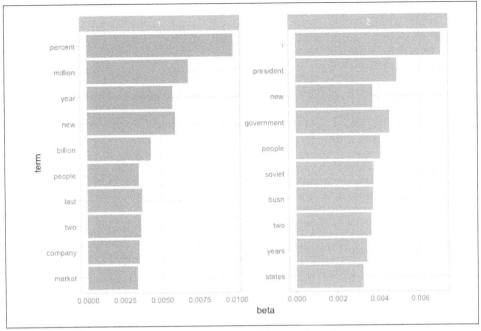

Figure 6-2. The terms that are most common within each topic

This visualization lets us understand the two topics that were extracted from the articles. The most common words in topic 1 include "percent," "million," "billion," and "company," which suggests it may represent business or financial news. Those most common in topic 2 include "president," "government," and "soviet," suggesting that this topic represents political news. One important observation about the words in each topic is that some words, such as "new" and "people," are common within both topics. This is an advantage of topic modeling as opposed to "hard clustering" methods: topics used in natural language could have some overlap in terms of words.

As an alternative, we could consider the terms that had the *greatest difference* in β between topic 1 and topic 2. This can be estimated based on the log ratio of the two:

$$\log_2 \left(\frac{\beta_2}{\beta_1} \right).$$

A log ratio is useful because it makes the difference symmetrical: β_2 being twice as large leads to a log ratio of 1, while β_1 being twice as large results in −1.

To constrain it to a set of especially relevant words, we can filter for relatively common words, such as those that have a β greater than 1/1000 in at least one topic.

```
library(tidyr)

beta_spread <- ap_topics %>%
  mutate(topic = paste0("topic", topic)) %>%
  spread(topic, beta) %>%
  filter(topic1 > .001 | topic2 > .001) %>%
  mutate(log_ratio = log2(topic2 / topic1))

beta_spread

## # A tibble: 198 × 4
##              term       topic1       topic2   log_ratio
##             <chr>        <dbl>        <dbl>       <dbl>
## 1  administration 4.309502e-04 1.382244e-03   1.6814189
## 2             ago 1.065216e-03 8.421279e-04  -0.3390353
## 3       agreement 6.714984e-04 1.039024e-03   0.6297728
## 4             aid 4.759043e-05 1.045958e-03   4.4580091
## 5             air 2.136933e-03 2.966593e-04  -2.8486628
## 6        american 2.030497e-03 1.683884e-03  -0.2700405
## 7         analysts 1.087581e-03 5.779708e-07 -10.8778386
## 8            area 1.371397e-03 2.310280e-04  -2.5695069
## 9            army 2.622192e-04 1.048089e-03   1.9989152
## 10          asked 1.885803e-04 1.559209e-03   3.0475641
## # ... with 188 more rows
```

The words with the greatest differences between the two topics are visualized in Figure 6-3.

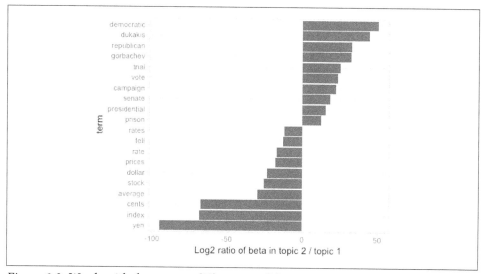

Figure 6-3. Words with the greatest difference in β between topic 2 and topic 1

We can see that the words more common in topic 2 include political parties such as "democratic" and "republican," as well as politician's names such as "dukakis" and "gorbachev." Topic 1 is more characterized by currencies like "yen" and "dollar," as well as financial terms such as "index," "prices," and "rates." This helps confirm that the two topics the algorithm identified are political and financial news.

Document-Topic Probabilities

Besides estimating each topic as a mixture of words, LDA also models each document as a mixture of topics. We can examine the per-document-per-topic probabilities, called γ ("gamma"), with the `matrix = "gamma"` argument to `tidy()`.

```
ap_documents <- tidy(ap_lda, matrix = "gamma")
ap_documents
```

```
## # A tibble: 4,492 × 3
##    document topic       gamma
##       <int> <int>       <dbl>
## 1         1     1 0.2480616686
## 2         2     1 0.3615485445
## 3         3     1 0.5265844180
## 4         4     1 0.3566530023
## 5         5     1 0.1812766762
## 6         6     1 0.0005883388
## 7         7     1 0.7734215655
## 8         8     1 0.0044516994
## 9         9     1 0.9669915139
## 10       10     1 0.1468904793
## # ... with 4,482 more rows
```

Each of these values is an estimated proportion of words from that document that are generated from that topic. For example, the model estimates that only about 24.8% of the words in document 1 are generated from topic 1.

We can see that many of these documents are drawn from a mix of the two topics, but that document 6 is drawn almost entirely from topic 2, having a γ from topic 1 close to zero. To check this answer, we could `tidy()` the document-term matrix (see "Tidy-ing a Document-Term Matrix" on page 70) and check what the most common words in that document are.

```
tidy(AssociatedPress) %>%
  filter(document == 6) %>%
  arrange(desc(count))
```

```
## # A tibble: 287 × 3
##    document           term count
##       <int>          <chr> <dbl>
## 1         6        noriega    16
## 2         6         panama    12
## 3         6        jackson     6
## 4         6         powell     6
## 5         6 administration     5
## 6         6       economic     5
```

```
## 7             6      general    5
## 8             6            i    5
## 9             6    panamanian    5
## 10            6     american    4
## # ... with 277 more rows
```

Based on the most common words, this appears to be an article about the relationship between the American government and Panamanian dictator Manuel Noriega, which means the algorithm was right to place it in topic 2 (as political/national news).

Example: The Great Library Heist

When examining a statistical method, it can be useful to try it on a very simple case where you know the "right answer." For example, we could collect a set of documents that definitely relate to four separate topics, then perform topic modeling to see whether the algorithm can correctly distinguish the four groups. This lets us double-check that the method is useful, and gain a sense of how and when it can go wrong. We'll try this with some data from classic literature.

Suppose a vandal has broken into your study and torn apart four of your books:

- *Great Expectations* by Charles Dickens
- *The War of the Worlds* by H.G. Wells
- *Twenty Thousand Leagues Under the Sea* by Jules Verne
- *Pride and Prejudice* by Jane Austen

This vandal has torn the books into individual chapters, and left them in one large pile. How can we restore these disorganized chapters to their original books? This is a challenging problem since the individual chapters are *unlabeled*: we don't know what words might distinguish them into groups. We'll thus use topic modeling to discover how chapters cluster into distinct topics, each of them (presumably) representing one of the books.

We'll retrieve the text of these four books using the gutenbergr package introduced in Chapter 3.

```
titles <- c("Twenty Thousand Leagues under the Sea", "The War of the Worlds",
            "Pride and Prejudice", "Great Expectations")

library(gutenbergr)

books <- gutenberg_works(title %in% titles) %>%
  gutenberg_download(meta_fields = "title")
```

As preprocessing, we divide these into chapters, use tidytext's `unnest_tokens()` to separate them into words, then remove `stop_words`. We're treating every chapter as a separate "document," each with a name like `Great Expectations_1` or `Pride and`

Prejudice_11. (In other applications, each document might be one newspaper article, or one blog post).

```
library(stringr)

# divide into documents, each representing one chapter
reg <- regex("^chapter ", ignore_case = TRUE)
by_chapter <- books %>%
  group_by(title) %>%
  mutate(chapter = cumsum(str_detect(text, reg))) %>%
  ungroup() %>%
  filter(chapter > 0) %>%
  unite(document, title, chapter)

# split into words
by_chapter_word <- by_chapter %>%
  unnest_tokens(word, text)

# find document-word counts
word_counts <- by_chapter_word %>%
  anti_join(stop_words) %>%
  count(document, word, sort = TRUE) %>%
  ungroup()

word_counts
```

```
## # A tibble: 104,721 × 3
##                     document    word      n
##                        <chr>   <chr>  <int>
## 1     Great Expectations_57     joe     88
## 2      Great Expectations_7     joe     70
## 3     Great Expectations_17   biddy     63
## 4     Great Expectations_27     joe     58
## 5     Great Expectations_38 estella     58
## 6      Great Expectations_2     joe     56
## 7     Great Expectations_23  pocket     53
## 8     Great Expectations_15     joe     50
## 9     Great Expectations_18     joe     50
## 10 The War of the Worlds_16 brother     50
## # ... with 104,711 more rows
```

LDA on Chapters

Right now our data frame word_counts is in a tidy form, with one term per document
per row, but the topicmodels package requires a DocumentTermMatrix. As described
in "Casting Tidy Text Data into a Matrix" on page 77, we can cast a one-token-per-
row table into a DocumentTermMatrix with tidytext's cast_dtm().

```
chapters_dtm <- word_counts %>%
  cast_dtm(document, word, n)

chapters_dtm

## <<DocumentTermMatrix (documents: 193, terms: 18215)>>
## Non-/sparse entries: 104721/3410774
## Sparsity          : 97%
## Maximal term length: 19
## Weighting         : term frequency (tf)
```

We can then use the LDA() function to create a four-topic model. In this case we know we're looking for four topics because there are four books; in other problems we may need to try a few different values of k.

```
chapters_lda <- LDA(chapters_dtm, k = 4, control = list(seed = 1234))
chapters_lda

## A LDA_VEM topic model with 4 topics.
```

Much as we did on the Associated Press data, we can examine per-topic-per-word probabilities.

```
chapter_topics <- tidy(chapters_lda, matrix = "beta")
chapter_topics

## # A tibble: 72,860 × 3
##     topic   term        beta
##     <int>  <chr>       <dbl>
## 1      1     joe 5.830326e-17
## 2      2     joe 3.194447e-57
## 3      3     joe 4.162676e-24
## 4      4     joe 1.445030e-02
## 5      1   biddy 7.846976e-27
## 6      2   biddy 4.672244e-69
## 7      3   biddy 2.259711e-46
## 8      4   biddy 4.767972e-03
## 9      1 estella 3.827272e-06
## 10     2 estella 5.316964e-65
## # ... with 72,850 more rows
```

Notice that this has turned the model into a one-topic-per-term-per-row format. For each combination, the model computes the probability of that term being generated from that topic. For example, the term "joe" has an almost zero probability of being generated from topics 1, 2, or 3, but it makes up 1.45% of topic 4.

We could use dplyr's top_n() to find the top five terms within each topic.

```
top_terms <- chapter_topics %>%
  group_by(topic) %>%
  top_n(5, beta) %>%
  ungroup() %>%
  arrange(topic, -beta)
```

```
top_terms
```

```
## # A tibble: 20 × 3
##    topic      term        beta
##    <int>     <chr>       <dbl>
## 1      1 elizabeth 0.014107538
## 2      1     darcy 0.008814258
## 3      1      miss 0.008706741
## 4      1    bennet 0.006947431
## 5      1      jane 0.006497512
## 6      2   captain 0.015507696
## 7      2  nautilus 0.013050048
## 8      2       sea 0.008850073
## 9      2      nemo 0.008708397
## 10     2       ned 0.008030799
## 11     3    people 0.006797400
## 12     3  martians 0.006512569
## 13     3      time 0.005347115
## 14     3     black 0.005278302
## 15     3     night 0.004483143
## 16     4       joe 0.014450300
## 17     4      time 0.006847574
## 18     4       pip 0.006817363
## 19     4    looked 0.006365257
## 20     4      miss 0.006228387
```

This tidy output lends itself well to a ggplot2 visualization (Figure 6-4).

```
library(ggplot2)

top_terms %>%
  mutate(term = reorder(term, beta)) %>%
  ggplot(aes(term, beta, fill = factor(topic))) +
  geom_col(show.legend = FALSE) +
  facet_wrap(~ topic, scales = "free") +
  coord_flip()
```

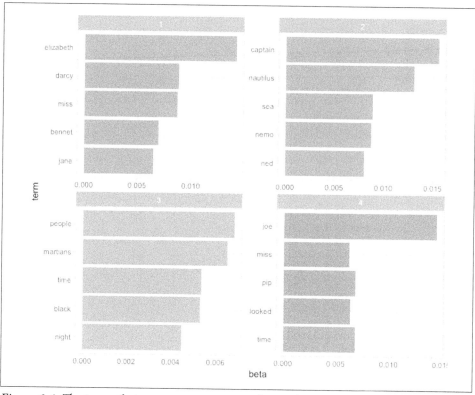

Figure 6-4. The terms that are most common within each topic

These topics are pretty clearly associated with the four books! There's no question that the topic of "captain," "nautilus," "sea," and "nemo" belongs to *Twenty Thousand Leagues Under the Sea*; and that "jane," "darcy," and "elizabeth" belongs to *Pride and Prejudice*. We see "pip" and "joe" from *Great Expectations*, and "martians," "black," and "night" from *The War of the Worlds*. We also notice that, in line with LDA being a "fuzzy clustering" method, there can be words in common between multiple topics, such as "miss" in topics 1 and 4, and "time" in topics 3 and 4.

Per-Document Classification

Each document in this analysis represented a single chapter. Thus, we may want to know which topics are associated with each document. Can we put the chapters back together in the correct books? We can find this by examining the per-document-per-topic probabilities, γ ("gamma").

```
chapters_gamma <- tidy(chapters_lda, matrix = "gamma")
chapters_gamma
```

```
## # A tibble: 772 × 3
##                       document topic         gamma
##                          <chr> <int>         <dbl>
## 1      Great Expectations_57       1 1.351886e-05
## 2       Great Expectations_7       1 1.470726e-05
## 3      Great Expectations_17       1 2.117127e-05
## 4      Great Expectations_27       1 1.919746e-05
## 5      Great Expectations_38       1 3.544403e-01
## 6       Great Expectations_2       1 1.723723e-05
## 7      Great Expectations_23       1 5.507241e-01
## 8      Great Expectations_15       1 1.682503e-02
## 9      Great Expectations_18       1 1.272044e-05
## 10 The War of the Worlds_16       1 1.084337e-05
## # ... with 762 more rows
```

Each of these values is an estimated proportion of words from that document that are generated from that topic. For example, the model estimates that each word in the Great Expectations_57 document has only a 0.00135% probability of coming from topic 1 (*Pride and Prejudice*).

Now that we have these topic probabilities, we can see how well our unsupervised learning did at distinguishing the four books. We'd expect that chapters within a book would be found to be mostly (or entirely) generated from the corresponding topic.

First we re-separate the document name into title and chapter, after which we can visualize the per-document-per-topic probability for each (Figure 6-5).

```
chapters_gamma <- chapters_gamma %>%
  separate(document, c("title", "chapter"), sep = "_", convert = TRUE)

chapters_gamma
```

```
## # A tibble: 772 × 4
##                    title chapter topic         gamma
## *                  <chr>   <int> <int>         <dbl>
## 1      Great Expectations      57       1 1.351886e-05
## 2      Great Expectations       7       1 1.470726e-05
## 3      Great Expectations      17       1 2.117127e-05
## 4      Great Expectations      27       1 1.919746e-05
## 5      Great Expectations      38       1 3.544403e-01
## 6      Great Expectations       2       1 1.723723e-05
## 7      Great Expectations      23       1 5.507241e-01
## 8      Great Expectations      15       1 1.682503e-02
## 9      Great Expectations      18       1 1.272044e-05
## 10 The War of the Worlds      16       1 1.084337e-05
## # ... with 762 more rows
```

```
# reorder titles in order of topic 1, topic 2, etc. before plotting
chapters_gamma %>%
  mutate(title = reorder(title, gamma * topic)) %>%
  ggplot(aes(factor(topic), gamma)) +
  geom_boxplot() +
  facet_wrap(~ title)
```

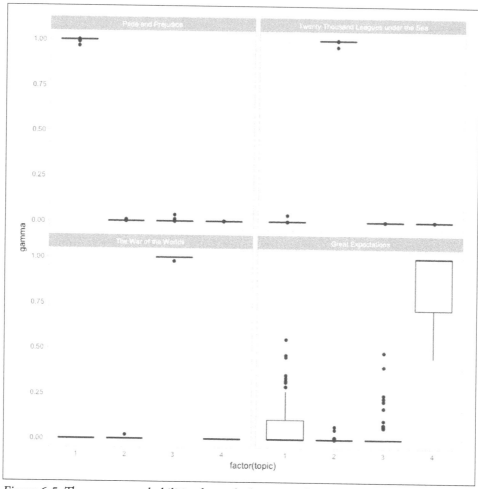

Figure 6-5. The gamma probabilities for each chapter within each book

We notice that almost all of the chapters from *Pride and Prejudice*, *The War of the Worlds*, and *Twenty Thousand Leagues Under the Sea* were uniquely identified as a single topic each.

It does look like some chapters from *Great Expectations* (which should be topic 4) were somewhat associated with other topics. Are there any cases where the topic most associated with a chapter belonged to another book? First we'd find the topic that was most associated with each chapter using top_n(), which is effectively the "classification" of that chapter.

```
chapter_classifications <- chapters_gamma %>%
  group_by(title, chapter) %>%
  top_n(1, gamma) %>%
```

```
ungroup()

chapter_classifications
```

```
## # A tibble: 193 × 4
##                    title chapter topic     gamma
##                    <chr>   <int> <int>     <dbl>
## 1    Great Expectations      23     1 0.5507241
## 2   Pride and Prejudice      43     1 0.9999610
## 3   Pride and Prejudice      18     1 0.9999654
## 4   Pride and Prejudice      45     1 0.9999038
## 5   Pride and Prejudice      16     1 0.9999466
## 6   Pride and Prejudice      29     1 0.9999300
## 7   Pride and Prejudice      10     1 0.9999203
## 8   Pride and Prejudice       8     1 0.9999134
## 9   Pride and Prejudice      56     1 0.9999337
## 10  Pride and Prejudice      47     1 0.9999506
## # ... with 183 more rows
```

We can then compare each to the "consensus" topic for each book (the most common topic among its chapters), and see which were most often misidentified.

```
book_topics <- chapter_classifications %>%
  count(title, topic) %>%
  group_by(title) %>%
  top_n(1, n) %>%
  ungroup() %>%
  transmute(consensus = title, topic)

chapter_classifications %>%
  inner_join(book_topics, by = "topic") %>%
  filter(title != consensus)
```

```
## # A tibble: 2 × 5
##                 title chapter topic     gamma           consensus
##                 <chr>   <int> <int>     <dbl>               <chr>
## 1 Great Expectations      23     1 0.5507241   Pride and Prejudice
## 2 Great Expectations      54     3 0.4803234 The War of the Worlds
```

We see that only two chapters from *Great Expectations* were misclassified, as LDA described one as coming from the *Pride and Prejudice* topic (topic 1) and one from *The War of the Worlds* (topic 3). That's not bad for unsupervised clustering!

By-Word Assignments: augment

One step of the LDA algorithm is assigning each word in each document to a topic. The more words in a document are assigned to that topic, generally, the more weight (gamma) will go on that document-topic classification.

We may want to take the original document-word pairs and find which words in each document were assigned to which topic. This is the job of the augment() function, which also originated in the broom package as a way of tidying model output. While `tidy()` retrieves the statistical components of the model, `augment()` uses a model to add information to each observation in the original data.

```
assignments <- augment(chapters_lda, data = chapters_dtm)
assignments

## # A tibble: 104,721 × 4
##                      document  term count .topic
##                         <chr> <chr> <dbl>  <dbl>
## 1   Great Expectations_57      joe    88      4
## 2    Great Expectations_7      joe    70      4
## 3   Great Expectations_17      joe     5      4
## 4   Great Expectations_27      joe    58      4
## 5    Great Expectations_2      joe    56      4
## 6   Great Expectations_23      joe     1      4
## 7   Great Expectations_15      joe    50      4
## 8   Great Expectations_18      joe    50      4
## 9    Great Expectations_9      joe    44      4
## 10  Great Expectations_13      joe    40      4
## # ... with 104,711 more rows
```

This returns a tidy data frame of book-term counts, but adds an extra column, `.topic`, with the topic each term was assigned to within each document. (Extra columns added by `augment` always start with `.` to prevent overwriting existing columns.) We can combine this `assignments` table with the consensus book titles to find which words were incorrectly classified.

```
assignments <- assignments %>%
  separate(document, c("title", "chapter"), sep = "_", convert = TRUE) %>%
  inner_join(book_topics, by = c(".topic" = "topic"))

assignments

## # A tibble: 104,721 × 6
##                 title chapter  term count .topic          consensus
##                 <chr>   <int> <chr> <dbl>  <dbl>              <chr>
## 1   Great Expectations      57   joe    88      4 Great Expectations
## 2   Great Expectations       7   joe    70      4 Great Expectations
## 3   Great Expectations      17   joe     5      4 Great Expectations
## 4   Great Expectations      27   joe    58      4 Great Expectations
## 5   Great Expectations       2   joe    56      4 Great Expectations
## 6   Great Expectations      23   joe     1      4 Great Expectations
## 7   Great Expectations      15   joe    50      4 Great Expectations
## 8   Great Expectations      18   joe    50      4 Great Expectations
## 9   Great Expectations       9   joe    44      4 Great Expectations
## 10  Great Expectations      13   joe    40      4 Great Expectations
## # ... with 104,711 more rows
```

This combination of the true book (`title`) and the book assigned to it (`consensus`) is useful for further exploration. We can, for example, visualize a *confusion matrix*, showing how often words from one book were assigned to another, using dplyr's `count()` and ggplot2's `geom_tile` (Figure 6-6).

```
assignments %>%
  count(title, consensus, wt = count) %>%
  group_by(title) %>%
  mutate(percent = n / sum(n)) %>%
  ggplot(aes(consensus, title, fill = percent)) +
  geom_tile() +
  scale_fill_gradient2(high = "red", label = percent_format()) +
  theme_minimal() +
  theme(axis.text.x = element_text(angle = 90, hjust = 1),
        panel.grid = element_blank()) +
  labs(x = "Book words were assigned to",
       y = "Book words came from",
       fill = "% of assignments")
```

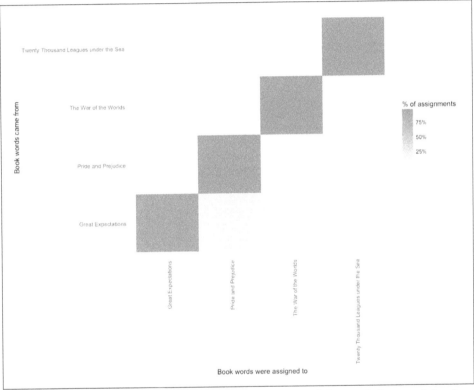

Figure 6-6. Confusion matrix showing where LDA assigned the words from each book. Each row of this table represents the true book each word came from, and each column represents what book it was assigned to.

We notice that almost all the words for *Pride and Prejudice*, *Twenty Thousand Leagues Under the Sea*, and *The War of the Worlds* were correctly assigned, while *Great Expectations* had a fair number of misassigned words (which, as we saw above, led to two chapters getting misclassified).

What were the most commonly mistaken words?

```
wrong_words <- assignments %>%
  filter(title != consensus)

wrong_words
```

```
## # A tibble: 4,535 × 6
##                                    title chapter      term count .topic
##                                    <chr>   <int>     <chr> <dbl>  <dbl>
## 1                      Great Expectations      38   brother     2      1
## 2                      Great Expectations      22   brother     4      1
## 3                      Great Expectations      23      miss     2      1
## 4                      Great Expectations      22      miss    23      1
## 5   Twenty Thousand Leagues under the Sea       8      miss     1      1
## 6                      Great Expectations      31      miss     1      1
## 7                      Great Expectations       5  sergeant    37      1
## 8                      Great Expectations      46   captain     1      2
## 9                      Great Expectations      32   captain     1      2
## 10            The War of the Worlds            17   captain     5      2
##                                   consensus
##                                       <chr>
## 1                        Pride and Prejudice
## 2                        Pride and Prejudice
## 3                        Pride and Prejudice
## 4                        Pride and Prejudice
## 5                        Pride and Prejudice
## 6                        Pride and Prejudice
## 7                        Pride and Prejudice
## 8    Twenty Thousand Leagues under the Sea
## 9    Twenty Thousand Leagues under the Sea
## 10   Twenty Thousand Leagues under the Sea
## # ... with 4,525 more rows
```

```
wrong_words %>%
  count(title, consensus, term, wt = count) %>%
  ungroup() %>%
  arrange(desc(n))
```

```
## # A tibble: 3,500 × 4
##                  title            consensus      term      n
##                  <chr>                <chr>     <chr>  <dbl>
## 1   Great Expectations  Pride and Prejudice      love     44
## 2   Great Expectations  Pride and Prejudice  sergeant     37
## 3   Great Expectations  Pride and Prejudice      lady     32
## 4   Great Expectations  Pride and Prejudice      miss     26
## 5   Great Expectations The War of the Worlds     boat     25
## 6   Great Expectations  Pride and Prejudice    father     19
## 7   Great Expectations The War of the Worlds    water     19
## 8   Great Expectations  Pride and Prejudice      baby     18
## 9   Great Expectations  Pride and Prejudice   flopson     18
## 10  Great Expectations  Pride and Prejudice    family     16
## # ... with 3,490 more rows
```

We can see that a number of words were often assigned to the *Pride and Prejudice* or *War of the Worlds* cluster even when they appeared in *Great Expectations*. For some of these words, such as "love" and "lady," that's because they're more common in *Pride and Prejudice* (we could confirm that by examining the counts).

On the other hand, there are a few wrongly classified words that never appeared in the novel they were misassigned to. For example, we can confirm "flopson" appears only in *Great Expectations*, even though it's assigned to the *Pride and Prejudice* cluster.

```
word_counts %>%
  filter(word == "flopson")

## # A tibble: 3 × 3
##                   document     word     n
##                     <chr>    <chr> <int>
## 1 Great Expectations_22 flopson    10
## 2 Great Expectations_23 flopson     7
## 3 Great Expectations_33 flopson     1
```

The LDA algorithm is stochastic, and it can accidentally land on a topic that spans multiple books.

Alternative LDA Implementations

The LDA() function in the topicmodels package is only one implementation of the latent Dirichlet allocation algorithm. For example, the mallet (*https://cran.r-project.org/package=mallet*) package (Mimno 2013) implements a wrapper around the MALLET (*http://mallet.cs.umass.edu/*) Java package for text classification tools, and the tidytext package provides tidiers for this model output as well.

The mallet package takes a somewhat different approach to the input format. For instance, it takes nontokenized documents and performs the tokenization itself, and requires a separate file of stop words. This means we have to collapse the text into one string for each document before performing LDA.

```
library(mallet)

# create a vector with one string per chapter
collapsed <- by_chapter_word %>%
  anti_join(stop_words, by = "word") %>%
  mutate(word = str_replace(word, "'", "")) %>%
  group_by(document) %>%
  summarize(text = paste(word, collapse = " "))

# create an empty file of "stop words"
file.create(empty_file <- tempfile())
docs <- mallet.import(collapsed$document, collapsed$text, empty_file)

mallet_model <- MalletLDA(num.topics = 4)
```

```
mallet_model$loadDocuments(docs)
mallet_model$train(100)
```

Once the model is created, however, we can use the `tidy()` and `augment()` functions described in the rest of the chapter in an almost identical way. This includes extracting the probabilities of words within each topic or topics within each document.

```
# word-topic pairs
tidy(mallet_model)

# document-topic pairs
tidy(mallet_model, matrix = "gamma")

# column needs to be named "term" for "augment"
term_counts <- rename(word_counts, term = word)
augment(mallet_model, term_counts)
```

We could use ggplot2 to explore and visualize the model in the same way we did the LDA output.

Summary

This chapter introduced topic modeling for finding clusters of words that characterize a set of documents, and showed how the `tidy()` verb lets us explore and understand these models using dplyr and ggplot2. This is one of the advantages of the tidy approach to model exploration: the challenges of different output formats are handled by the tidying functions, and we can explore model results using a standard set of tools. In particular, we saw that topic modeling is able to separate and distinguish chapters from four separate books, and explored the limitations of the model by finding words and chapters that it assigned incorrectly.

## CHAPTER 7

Case Study: Comparing Twitter Archives

One type of text that gets plenty of attention is text shared online via Twitter. In fact, several of the sentiment lexicons used in this book (and commonly used in general) were designed for use with and validated on tweets. Both authors of this book are on Twitter and are fairly regular users of it, so in this case study, let's compare the entire Twitter archives of Julia (*https://twitter.com/juliasilge*) and David (*https://twitter.com/drob*).

Getting the Data and Distribution of Tweets

An individual can download his or her own Twitter archive by following directions available on Twitter's website (*https://support.twitter.com/articles/20170160*). We each downloaded ours and will now open them up. Let's use the lubridate package to convert the string timestamps to date-time objects and initially take a look at our tweeting patterns overall (Figure 7-1).

```
library(lubridate)
library(ggplot2)
library(dplyr)
library(readr)

tweets_julia <- read_csv("data/tweets_julia.csv")
tweets_dave <- read_csv("data/tweets_dave.csv")
tweets <- bind_rows(tweets_julia %>%
                        mutate(person = "Julia"),
                    tweets_dave %>%
                        mutate(person = "David")) %>%
  mutate(timestamp = ymd_hms(timestamp))

ggplot(tweets, aes(x = timestamp, fill = person)) +
  geom_histogram(position = "identity", bins = 20, show.legend = FALSE) +
  facet_wrap(~person, ncol = 1)
```

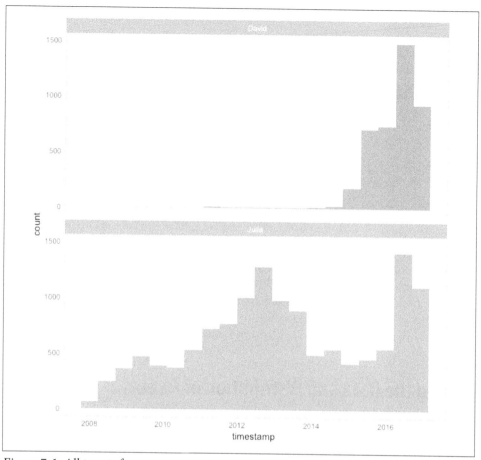

Figure 7-1. All tweets from our accounts

David and Julia tweet at about the same rate currently and joined Twitter about a year apart from each other, but there were about five years where David was not active on Twitter and Julia was. In total, Julia has about four times as many tweets as David.

Word Frequencies

Let's use unnest_tokens() to make a tidy data frame of all the words in our tweets, and remove the common English stop words. There are certain conventions in how people use text on Twitter, so we will do a bit more work with our text here than, for example, we did with the narrative text from Project Gutenberg.

First, we will remove tweets from this dataset that are retweets so that we only have tweets that we wrote ourselves. Next, the mutate() line removes links and cleans out some characters that we don't want, like ampersands and such.

In the call to `unnest_tokens()`, we unnest using a regex pattern, instead of just looking for single unigrams (words). This regex pattern is very useful for dealing with Twitter text; it retains hashtags and mentions of usernames with the @ symbol.

Because we have kept these types of symbols in the text, we can't use a simple `anti_join()` to remove stop words. Instead, we can take the approach shown in the `filter()` line that uses `str_detect()` from the stringr package.

```
library(tidytext)
library(stringr)

replace_reg1 <- "https://t.co/[A-Za-z\\d]+|"
replace_reg2 <- "http://[A-Za-z\\d]+|&amp;|&lt;|&gt;|RT|https"
replace_reg <- paste0(replace_reg1, replace_reg2)
unnest_reg <- "([^A-Za-z_\\d#@']|'(?![A-Za-z_\\d#@]))"
tidy_tweets <- tweets %>%
  filter(!str_detect(text, "^RT")) %>%
  mutate(text = str_replace_all(text, replace_reg, "")) %>%
  unnest_tokens(word, text, token = "regex", pattern = unnest_reg) %>%
  filter(!word %in% stop_words$word,
         str_detect(word, "[a-z]"))
```

Now we can calculate word frequencies for each person. First, we group by person and count how many times each person used each word. Then we use `left_join()` to add a column of the total number of words used by each person. (This is higher for Julia than David since she has more tweets than David.) Finally, we calculate a frequency for each person and word.

```
frequency <- tidy_tweets %>%
  group_by(person) %>%
  count(word, sort = TRUE) %>%
  left_join(tidy_tweets %>%
              group_by(person) %>%
              summarise(total = n())) %>%
  mutate(freq = n/total)

frequency
```

```
## Source: local data frame [20,736 x 5]
## Groups: person [2]
##
##     person            word      n total         freq
##      <chr>           <chr>  <int> <int>        <dbl>
## 1    Julia            time    584 74572 0.007831358
## 2    Julia     @selkie1970    570 74572 0.007643620
## 3    Julia        @skedman    531 74572 0.007120635
## 4    Julia             day    467 74572 0.006262404
## 5    Julia            baby    408 74572 0.005471222
## 6    David @hadleywickham    315 20161 0.015624225
## 7    Julia            love    304 74572 0.004076597
```

```
## 8    Julia   @haleynburke    299 74572 0.004009548
## 9    Julia          house    289 74572 0.003875449
## 10   Julia        morning    278 74572 0.003727941
## # ... with 20,726 more rows
```

This is a nice and tidy data frame, but we would actually like to plot those frequencies on the x- and y-axes of a plot, so we will need to use spread() from tidyr to make a differently shaped data frame.

```
library(tidyr)

frequency <- frequency %>%
  select(person, word, freq) %>%
  spread(person, freq) %>%
  arrange(Julia, David)

frequency
```

```
## # A tibble: 17,640 × 3
##                   word         David        Julia
##                  <chr>         <dbl>        <dbl>
## 1                   's 4.960071e-05 1.340986e-05
## 2     @accidental__art 4.960071e-05 1.340986e-05
## 3          @alice_data 4.960071e-05 1.340986e-05
## 4           @alistaire 4.960071e-05 1.340986e-05
## 5          @corynissen 4.960071e-05 1.340986e-05
## 6      @jennybryan's 4.960071e-05 1.340986e-05
## 7             @jsvine 4.960071e-05 1.340986e-05
## 8        @lizasperling 4.960071e-05 1.340986e-05
## 9          @ognyanova 4.960071e-05 1.340986e-05
## 10         @rbloggers 4.960071e-05 1.340986e-05
## # ... with 17,630 more rows
```

Now this is ready for us to plot. Let's use geom_jitter() so that we don't see the discreteness at the low end of frequency as much, and check_overlap = TRUE so the text labels don't all print out on top of each other (only some will print; see Figure 7-2).

```
library(scales)

ggplot(frequency, aes(Julia, David)) +
  geom_jitter(alpha = 0.1, size = 2.5, width = 0.25, height = 0.25) +
  geom_text(aes(label = word), check_overlap = TRUE, vjust = 1.5) +
  scale_x_log10(labels = percent_format()) +
  scale_y_log10(labels = percent_format()) +
  geom_abline(color = "red")
```

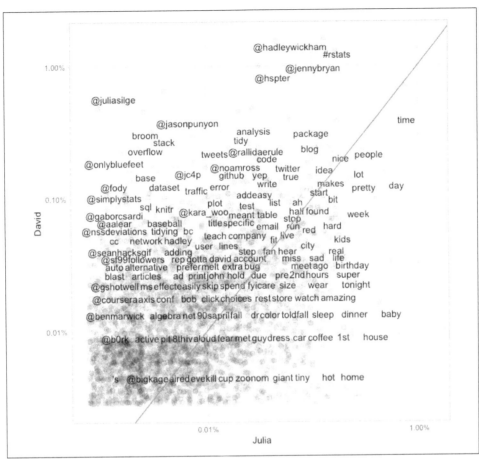

Figure 7-2. Comparing the frequency of words used by Julia and David

Words near the line in Figure 7-2 are used with about equal frequencies by David and Julia, while words far away from the line are used much more by one person compared to the other. Words, hashtags, and usernames that appear in this plot are ones that we have both used at least once in tweets.

This may not even need to be pointed out, but David and Julia have used their Twitter accounts rather differently over the course of the past several years. David has used his Twitter account almost exclusively for professional purposes since he became more active, while Julia used it for entirely personal purposes until late 2015 and still uses it more personally than David. We see these differences immediately in this plot exploring word frequencies, and they will continue to be obvious in the rest of this chapter.

Comparing Word Usage

We just made a plot comparing raw word frequencies over our whole Twitter histories; now let's find which words are more or less likely to come from each person's account using the log odds ratio. First, let's restrict the analysis moving forward to tweets from David and Julia sent during 2016. David was consistently active on Twitter for all of 2016, and this was about when Julia transitioned into data science as a career.

```
tidy_tweets <- tidy_tweets %>%
  filter(timestamp >= as.Date("2016-01-01"),
         timestamp < as.Date("2017-01-01"))
```

Next, let's use `str_detect()` to remove Twitter usernames from the word column, because otherwise, the results here are dominated only by people who Julia or David know and the other does not. After removing these, we count how many times each person uses each word and keep only the words used more than 10 times. After a `spread()` operation, we can calculate the log odds ratio for each word, using:

$$\text{log odds ratio} = \ln\left(\frac{\left[\frac{n+1}{\text{total}+1}\right]_{\text{David}}}{\left[\frac{n+1}{\text{total}+1}\right]_{\text{Julia}}}\right)$$

where n is the number of times the word in question is used by each person, and the total indicates the total words for each person.

```
word_ratios <- tidy_tweets %>%
  filter(!str_detect(word, "^@")) %>%
  count(word, person) %>%
  filter(sum(n) >= 10) %>%
  ungroup() %>%
  spread(person, n, fill = 0) %>%
  mutate_if(is.numeric, funs((. + 1) / sum(. + 1))) %>%
  mutate(logratio = log(David / Julia)) %>%
  arrange(desc(logratio))
```

What are some words that have been about equally likely to come from David's or Julia's account during 2016?

```
word_ratios %>%
  arrange(abs(logratio))
```

```
## # A tibble: 377 × 4
##         word      David      Julia    logratio
##        <chr>      <dbl>      <dbl>       <dbl>
## 1        map 0.002321655 0.002314815 0.002950476
## 2      email 0.002110595 0.002083333 0.013000812
## 3       file 0.002110595 0.002083333 0.013000812
## 4      names 0.003799071 0.003703704 0.025423332
```

```
## 5       account 0.001688476 0.001620370 0.041171689
## 6           api 0.001688476 0.001620370 0.041171689
## 7      function 0.003376952 0.003240741 0.041171689
## 8    population 0.001688476 0.001620370 0.041171689
## 9           sad 0.001688476 0.001620370 0.041171689
## 10        words 0.003376952 0.003240741 0.041171689
## # ... with 367 more rows
```

We are about equally likely to tweet about maps, email, APIs, and functions.

Which words are most likely to be from Julia's account or from David's account? Let's just take the top 15 most distinctive words for each account and plot them in Figure 7-3.

```
word_ratios %>%
  group_by(logratio < 0) %>%
  top_n(15, abs(logratio)) %>%
  ungroup() %>%
  mutate(word = reorder(word, logratio)) %>%
  ggplot(aes(word, logratio, fill = logratio < 0)) +
  geom_col(show.legend = FALSE) +
  coord_flip() +
  ylab("log odds ratio (David/Julia)") +
  scale_fill_discrete(name = "", labels = c("David", "Julia"))
```

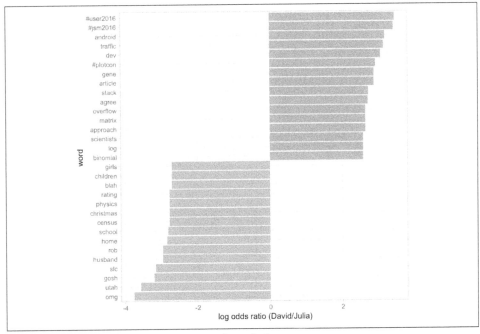

Figure 7-3. Comparing the odds ratios of words from our accounts

So David has tweeted about specific conferences he has gone to, genes, Stack Over-flow, and matrices; while Julia tweeted about Utah, physics, Census data, Christmas, and her family.

Changes in Word Use

The section above looked at overall word use, but now let's ask a different question. Which words' frequencies have changed the fastest in our Twitter feeds? Or to state this another way, which words have we tweeted about at a higher or lower rate as time has passed? To do this, we will define a new time variable in the data frame that defines which unit of time each tweet was posted in. We can use floor_date() from lubridate to do this, with a unit of our choosing; using 1 month seems to work well for this year of tweets from both of us.

After we have the time bins defined, we count how many times each of us used each word in each time bin. After that, we add columns to the data frame for the total number of words used in each time bin by each person and the total number of times each word was used by each person. We can then filter() to only keep words used at least some minimum number of times (30, in this case).

```
words_by_time <- tidy_tweets %>%
  filter(!str_detect(word, "^@")) %>%
  mutate(time_floor = floor_date(timestamp, unit = "1 month")) %>%
  count(time_floor, person, word) %>%
  ungroup() %>%
  group_by(person, time_floor) %>%
  mutate(time_total = sum(n)) %>%
  group_by(word) %>%
  mutate(word_total = sum(n)) %>%
  ungroup() %>%
  rename(count = n) %>%
  filter(word_total > 30)

words_by_time
```

```
## # A tibble: 970 × 6
##       time_floor person    word count time_total word_total
##           <dttm>  <chr>   <chr> <int>      <int>      <int>
## 1  2016-01-01  David #rstats     2        307        324
## 2  2016-01-01  David     bad     1        307         33
## 3  2016-01-01  David     bit     2        307         45
## 4  2016-01-01  David    blog     1        307         60
## 5  2016-01-01  David   broom     2        307         41
## 6  2016-01-01  David    call     2        307         31
## 7  2016-01-01  David   check     1        307         42
## 8  2016-01-01  David    code     3        307         49
## 9  2016-01-01  David    data     2        307        276
## 10 2016-01-01  David     day     2        307         65
## # ... with 960 more rows
```

Each row in this data frame corresponds to one person using one word in a given time bin. The `count` column tells us how many times that person used that word in that time bin, the `time_total` column tells us how many words that person used during that time bin, and the `word_total` column tells us how many times that person used that word over the whole year. This is the data set we can use for modeling.

We can use `nest()` from tidyr to make a data frame with a list column that contains little miniature data frames for each word. Let's do that now and take a look at the resulting structure.

```
nested_data <- words_by_time %>%
  nest(-word, -person)

nested_data

## # A tibble: 112 × 3
##    person  word            data
##    <chr>   <chr>         <list>
## 1  David  #rstats <tibble [12 × 4]>
## 2  David      bad <tibble [9 × 4]>
## 3  David      bit <tibble [10 × 4]>
## 4  David     blog <tibble [12 × 4]>
## 5  David    broom <tibble [10 × 4]>
## 6  David     call <tibble [9 × 4]>
## 7  David    check <tibble [12 × 4]>
## 8  David     code <tibble [10 × 4]>
## 9  David     data <tibble [12 × 4]>
## 10 David      day <tibble [8 × 4]>
## # ... with 102 more rows
```

This data frame has one row for each person-word combination; the `data` column is a list column that contains data frames, one for each combination of person and word. Let's use `map()` from the purrr library to apply our modeling procedure to each of those little data frames inside our big data frame. This is count data, so let's use `glm()` with `family = "binomial"` for modeling.

```
library(purrr)

nested_models <- nested_data %>%
  mutate(models = map(data, ~ glm(cbind(count, time_total) ~ time_floor, .,
                                  family = "binomial")))

nested_models

## # A tibble: 112 × 4
##    person  word            data     models
##    <chr>   <chr>         <list>     <list>
## 1  David  #rstats <tibble [12 × 4]> <S3: glm>
## 2  David      bad <tibble [9 × 4]> <S3: glm>
## 3  David      bit <tibble [10 × 4]> <S3: glm>
## 4  David     blog <tibble [12 × 4]> <S3: glm>
```

```
## 5    David   broom <tibble [10 × 4]> <S3: glm>
## 6    David    call <tibble [9 × 4]> <S3: glm>
## 7    David   check <tibble [12 × 4]> <S3: glm>
## 8    David    code <tibble [10 × 4]> <S3: glm>
## 9    David    data <tibble [12 × 4]> <S3: glm>
## 10   David     day <tibble [8 × 4]> <S3: glm>
## # ... with 102 more rows
```

 We can think about this modeling procedure answering questions like, "Was a given word mentioned in a given time bin? Yes or no? How does the count of word mentions depend on time?"

Now notice that we have a new column for the modeling results; it is another list column and contains glm objects. The next step is to use map() and tidy() from the broom package to pull out the slopes for each of these models and find the important ones. We are comparing many slopes here, and some of them are not statistically significant, so let's apply an adjustment to the p-values for multiple comparisons.

```
library(broom)

slopes <- nested_models %>%
  unnest(map(models, tidy)) %>%
  filter(term == "time_floor") %>%
  mutate(adjusted.p.value = p.adjust(p.value))
```

Now let's find the most important slopes. Which words have changed in frequency at a moderately significant level in our tweets?

```
top_slopes <- slopes %>%
  filter(adjusted.p.value < 0.1) %>%
  select(-statistic, -p.value)

top_slopes
```

```
## # A tibble: 6 × 8
##    person      word      term      estimate    std.error adjusted.p.value
##     <chr>     <chr>     <chr>         <dbl>        <dbl>            <dbl>
## 1   David   ggplot2 time_floor -8.262540e-08 1.969448e-08     2.996837e-03
## 2   Julia    #rstats time_floor -4.496395e-08 1.119780e-08     6.467858e-03
## 3   Julia       post time_floor -4.818545e-08 1.454440e-08     9.784245e-02
## 4   Julia       read time_floor -9.327168e-08 2.542485e-08     2.634712e-02
## 5   David      stack time_floor  8.041202e-08 2.193375e-08     2.634841e-02
## 6   David #user2016 time_floor -8.175896e-07 1.550152e-07     1.479603e-05
```

To visualize our results, we can plot the use of these words for both David and Julia over this year of tweets (Figure 7-4).

```
words_by_time %>%
  inner_join(top_slopes, by = c("word", "person")) %>%
  filter(person == "David") %>%
```

```
ggplot(aes(time_floor, count/time_total, color = word, lty = word)) +
geom_line(size = 1.3) +
labs(x = NULL, y = "Word frequency")
```

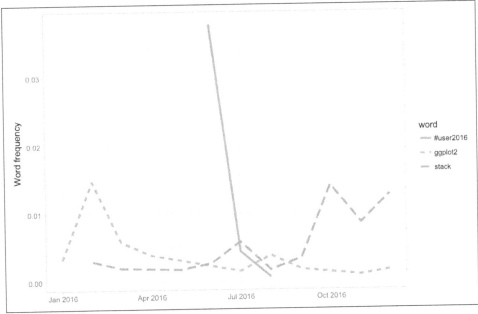

Figure 7-4. Trending words in David's tweets

We see in Figure 7-4 that David tweeted a lot about the UseR conference while he was there and then quickly stopped. He has tweeted more about Stack Overflow toward the end of the year and less about ggplot2 (*http://bit.ly/2qXj5aI*) as the year has progressed.

Now let's plot words that have changed frequency in Julia's tweets in Figure 7-5.

```
words_by_time %>%
  inner_join(top_slopes, by = c("word", "person")) %>%
  filter(person == "Julia") %>%
  ggplot(aes(time_floor, count/time_total, color = word, lty = word)) +
  geom_line(size = 1.3) +
  labs(x = NULL, y = "Word frequency")
```

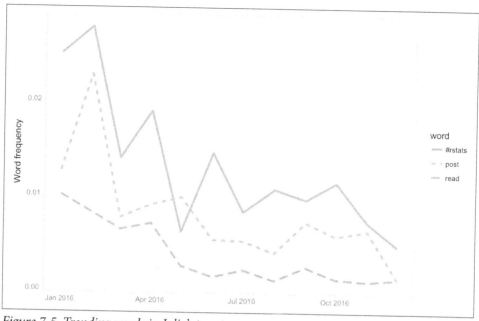

Figure 7-5. Trending words in Julia's tweets

All the significant slopes for Julia are negative. This means she has not tweeted at a higher rate using any specific words, but instead used a variety of different words; her tweets earlier in the year contained the words shown in this plot at higher proportions. Words she uses when publicizing a new blog post, like the #rstats hashtag and "post," have gone down in frequency, and she has tweeted less about reading.

Favorites and Retweets

Another important characteristic of tweets is how many times they are favorited or retweeted. Let's explore which words are more likely to be retweeted or favorited for Julia's and David's tweets. When a user downloads his or her own Twitter archive, favorites and retweets are not included, so we constructed another dataset of the authors' tweets that includes this information. We accessed our own tweets via the Twitter API and downloaded about 3,200 tweets for each person. In both cases, that is about the last 18 months worth of Twitter activity. This corresponds to a period of increasing activity and increasing numbers of followers for both of us.

```
tweets_julia <- read_csv("data/juliasilge_tweets.csv")
tweets_dave <- read_csv("data/drob_tweets.csv")
tweets <- bind_rows(tweets_julia %>%
                        mutate(person = "Julia"),
                    tweets_dave %>%
                        mutate(person = "David")) %>%
    mutate(created_at = ymd_hms(created_at))
```

Now that we have this second, smaller set of only recent tweets, let's use unn est_tokens() to transform these tweets to a tidy data set. Let's remove all retweets and replies from this data set so we only look at regular tweets that David and Julia have posted directly.

```
tidy_tweet %>%
  select(-source)
  filter(!str_detect(text, "^(RT|@)")) %>%
  mutate(text = str_replace_all(text, replace_reg, "")) %>%
  unnest_tokens(word, text, token = "regex", pattern = unnest_reg) %>%
  anti_join(stop_words)

tidy_tweets
```

```
## # A tibble: 11,078 × 7
##               id        created_at retweets favorites person       word
##            <dbl>            <dttm>    <int>     <int>  <chr>       <chr>
## 1  8.044026e+17 2016-12-01 19:11:43        1        15  David       worry
## 2  8.043967e+17 2016-12-01 18:48:07        4         6  David         j's
## 3  8.043611e+17 2016-12-01 16:26:39        8        12  David   bangalore
## 4  8.043611e+17 2016-12-01 16:26:39        8        12  David      london
## 5  8.043611e+17 2016-12-01 16:26:39        8        12  David  developers
## 6  8.041571e+17 2016-12-01 02:56:10        0        11  Julia  management
## 7  8.041571e+17 2016-12-01 02:56:10        0        11  Julia       julie
## 8  8.040582e+17 2016-11-30 20:23:14       30        41  David          sf
## 9  8.040324e+17 2016-11-30 18:40:27        0        17  Julia      zipped
## 10 8.040324e+17 2016-11-30 18:40:27        0        17  Julia          gb
## # ... with 11,068 more rows
```

To start with, let's look at the number of times each of our tweets was retweeted. Let's find the total number of retweets for each person.

```
totals <- tidy_tweets %>%
  group_by(person, id) %>%
  summarise(rts = sum(retweets)) %>%
  group_by(person) %>%
  summarise(total_rts = sum(rts))

totals
```

```
## # A tibble: 2 × 2
##    person total_rts
##     <chr>     <int>
## 1  David    110171
## 2  Julia     12701
```

Now let's find the median number of retweets for each word and person. We probably want to count each tweet/word combination only once, so we will use group_by() and summarise() twice, one right after the other. The first summarise() statement counts how many times each word was retweeted, for each tweet and person. In the second summarise() statement, we can find the median retweets for each person and word, count the number of times each word was used by each person, and keep that in uses. Next, we can join this to the data frame of retweet totals. Let's `filter()` to only keep words mentioned at least five times.

```
word_by_rts <- tidy_tweets %>%
  group_by(id, word, person) %>%
  summarise(rts = first(retweets)) %>%
  group_by(person, word) %>%
  summarise(retweets = median(rts), uses = n()) %>%
  left_join(totals) %>%
  filter(retweets != 0) %>%
  ungroup()

word_by_rts %>%
  filter(uses >= 5) %>%
  arrange(desc(retweets))

## # A tibble: 178 × 5
##    person          word retweets  uses total_rts
##    <chr>          <chr>    <dbl> <int>     <int>
## 1  David      animation     85.0     5    110171
## 2  David       download     52.0     5    110171
## 3  David          start     51.0     7    110171
## 4  Julia       tidytext     50.0     7     12701
## 5  David       gganimate     45.0     8    110171
## 6  David    introducing     45.0     6    110171
## 7  David  understanding     37.0     6    110171
## 8  David              0     35.0     7    110171
## 9  David          error     34.5     8    110171
## 10 David       bayesian     34.0     7    110171
## # ... with 168 more rows
```

At the top of this sorted data frame, we see tweets from Julia and David about packages that they work on, like gutenbergr (*https://cran.r-project.org/package=guten bergr*), gganimate (*https://github.com/dgrtwo/gganimate*), and tidytext (*https://cran.r-project.org/package=tidytext*). Let's plot the words that have the highest median retweets for each of our accounts (Figure 7-6).

```
word_by_rts %>%
  filter(uses >= 5) %>%
  group_by(person) %>%
  top_n(10, retweets) %>%
  arrange(retweets) %>%
  ungroup() %>%
  mutate(word = factor(word, unique(word))) %>%
  ungroup() %>%
  ggplot(aes(word, retweets, fill = person)) +
  geom_col(show.legend = FALSE) +
  facet_wrap(~ person, scales = "free", ncol = 2) +
  coord_flip() +
  labs(x = NULL,
       y = "Median # of retweets for tweets containing each word")
```

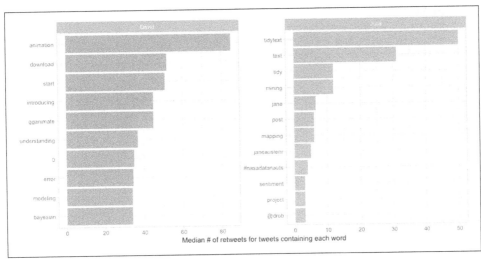

Figure 7-6. Words with highest median retweets

We see lots of words about R packages, including tidytext, a package about which you are reading right now! The "0" for David comes from tweets where he mentions version numbers of packages, like "broom 0.4.0" (*http://bit.ly/2qagcDI*) or similar.

We can follow a similar procedure to see which words led to more favorites. Are they different than the words that lead to more retweets?

```
totals <- tidy_tweets %>%
  group_by(person, id) %>%
  summarise(favs = sum(favorites)) %>%
  group_by(person) %>%
  summarise(total_favs = sum(favs))

word_by_favs <- tidy_tweets %>%
  group_by(id, word, person) %>%
  summarise(favs = first(favorites)) %>%
  group_by(person, word) %>%
  summarise(favorites = median(favs), uses = n()) %>%
  left_join(totals) %>%
  filter(favorites != 0) %>%
  ungroup()
```

We have built the data frames we need. Now let's make our visualization in Figure 7-7.

```
word_by_favs %>%
  filter(uses >= 5) %>%
  group_by(person) %>%
  top_n(10, favorites) %>%
  arrange(favorites) %>%
  ungroup() %>%
  mutate(word = factor(word, unique(word))) %>%
```

```
ungroup() %>%
ggplot(aes(word, favorites, fill = person)) +
geom_col(show.legend = FALSE) +
facet_wrap(~ person, scales = "free", ncol = 2) +
coord_flip() +
labs(x = NULL,
     y = "Median # of favorites for tweets containing each word")
```

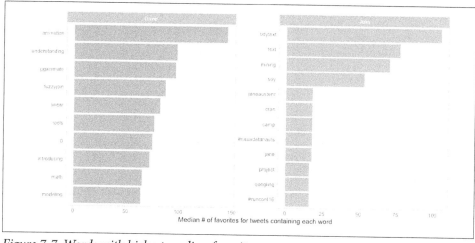

Figure 7-7. Words with highest median favorites

We see some minor differences between Figures 7-6 and 7-7, especially near the bottom of the top 10 list, but these are largely the same words as for retweets. In general, the same words that lead to retweets lead to favorites. A prominent word for Julia in both plots is the hashtag for the NASA Datanauts program that she has participated in; read on to Chapter 8 to learn more about NASA data and what we can learn from text analysis of NASA datasets.

Summary

This chapter was our first case study, a beginning-to-end analysis that demonstrated how to bring together the concepts and code we have been exploring in a cohesive way to understand a text data set. Comparing word frequencies allowed us to see which words we tweeted more and less frequently, and the log odds ratio showed which words are more likely to be tweeted from each of our accounts. We can use nest() and map() with the glm() function to find which words we have tweeted at higher and lower rates as time has passed. Finally, we can find which words in our tweets led to higher numbers of retweets and favorites. All of these are examples of approaches to measure how we use words in similar and different ways, and how the characteristics of our tweets are changing or compare with each other. These are flexible approaches to text mining that can be applied to other types of text as well.

## CHAPTER 8

Case Study: Mining NASA Metadata

There are over 32,000 datasets hosted and/or maintained by NASA (*https://www.nasa.gov/*); these datasets cover topics from Earth science to aerospace engineering to management of NASA itself. We can use the metadata for these datasets to understand the connections between them.

 What is metadata? Metadata is a term that refers to data that gives information about other data; in this case, the metadata informs users about what is in these numerous NASA datasets but does not include the content of the datasets themselves.

The metadata includes information like the title of the dataset, a description field, what organization(s) within NASA is responsible for the dataset, keywords for the dataset that have been assigned by a human being, and so forth. NASA places a high priority on making its data open and accessible, even requiring all NASA-funded research to be openly accessible online (*https://www.nasa.gov/press-release/nasa-unveils-new-public-web-portal-for-research-results*). The metadata for all its datasets is publicly available online in JSON format (*https://data.nasa.gov/data.json*).

In this chapter, we will treat the NASA metadata as a text dataset and show how to implement several tidy text approaches with this real-life text. We will use word co-occurrences and correlations, tf-idf, and topic modeling to explore the connections between the datasets. Can we find datasets that are related to each other? Can we find clusters of similar datasets? Since we have several text fields in the NASA metadata, most importantly the title, description, and keyword fields, we can explore the connections between the fields to better understand the complex world of data at NASA. This type of approach can be extended to any domain that deals with text, so let's take a look at this metadata and get started.

How Data Is Organized at NASA

First, let's download the JSON file and take a look at the names of what is stored in the metadata.

```
library(jsonlite)
metadata <- fromJSON("https://data.nasa.gov/data.json")
names(metadata$dataset)
```

```
##  [1] "_id"                "@type"            "accessLevel"
##  [4] "accrualPeriodicity" "bureauCode"       "contactPoint"
##  [7] "description"        "distribution"     "identifier"
## [10] "issued"             "keyword"          "landingPage"
## [13] "language"           "modified"         "programCode"
## [16] "publisher"          "spatial"          "temporal"
## [19] "theme"              "title"            "license"
## [22] "isPartOf"           "references"       "rights"
## [25] "describedBy"
```

We see here that we could extract information from who publishes each dataset to what license each dataset is released under.

It seems likely that the title, description, and keywords for each dataset may be most fruitful for drawing connections between datasets. Let's check them out.

```
class(metadata$dataset$title)
```

```
## [1] "character"
```

```
class(metadata$dataset$description)
```

```
## [1] "character"
```

```
class(metadata$dataset$keyword)
```

```
## [1] "list"
```

The title and description fields are stored as character vectors, but the keywords are stored as a list of character vectors.

Wrangling and Tidying the Data

Let's set up separate tidy data frames for title, description, and keyword, keeping the dataset IDs for each so that we can connect them later in the analysis if necessary.

```
library(dplyr)

nasa_title <- data_frame(id = metadata$dataset$`_id`$`$oid`,
                         title = metadata$dataset$title)
nasa_title
```

```
## # A tibble: 32,089 × 2
##                             id                             title
##                          <chr>                             <chr>
## 1   55942a57c63a7fe59b495a77       15 Minute Stream Flow Data: USGS (FIFE
```

```
## 2  55942a57c63a7fe59b495a78                    15 Minute Stream Flow Data: USGS (FIFE
## 3  55942a58c63a7fe59b495a79                    15 Minute Stream Flow Data: USGS (FIFE
## 4  55942a58c63a7fe59b495a7a 2000 Pilot Environmental Sustainability Index (ESI
## 5  55942a58c63a7fe59b495a7b 2000 Pilot Environmental Sustainability Index (ESI
## 6  55942a58c63a7fe59b495a7c 2000 Pilot Environmental Sustainability Index (ESI
## 7  55942a58c63a7fe59b495a7d      2001 Environmental Sustainability Index (ESI
## 8  55942a58c63a7fe59b495a7e      2001 Environmental Sustainability Index (ESI
## 9  55942a58c63a7fe59b495a7f      2001 Environmental Sustainability Index (ESI
## 10 55942a58c63a7fe59b495a80      2001 Environmental Sustainability Index (ESI
## # ... with 32,079 more rows
```

These are just a few example titles from the datasets we will be exploring. Notice that we have the NASA-assigned IDs here, and also that there are duplicate titles on separate datasets.

```
nasa_desc <- data_frame(id = metadata$dataset$`_id`$`$oid`,
                        desc = metadata$dataset$description)

nasa_desc %>%
  select(desc) %>%
  sample_n(5)

## # A tibble: 5 × 1
##
##
## 1 MODIS (or Moderate Resolution Imaging Spectroradiometer) is a key instrument
## 2                               Fatigue Countermeasures: A Meta-Ana
## 3  Mobile communications systems require programmable embedded platforms that
## 4  The Doppler Aerosol WiNd (DAWN), a pulsed lidar, operated aboard a NASA DC-
## 5 MODIS (or Moderate Resolution Imaging Spectroradiometer) is a key instrument
```

Here we see the first part of several selected description fields from the metadata.

Now we can build the tidy data frame for the keywords. For this one, we need to use unnest() from tidyr, because they are in a list-column.

```
library(tidyr)

nasa_keyword <- data_frame(id = metadata$dataset$`_id`$`$oid`,
                           keyword = metadata$dataset$keyword) %>%
  unnest(keyword)

nasa_keyword

## # A tibble: 126,814 × 2
##                            id       keyword
##                         <chr>         <chr>
## 1  55942a57c63a7fe59b495a77 EARTH SCIENCE
## 2  55942a57c63a7fe59b495a77    HYDROSPHERE
## 3  55942a57c63a7fe59b495a77 SURFACE WATER
## 4  55942a57c63a7fe59b495a78 EARTH SCIENCE
## 5  55942a57c63a7fe59b495a78    HYDROSPHERE
## 6  55942a57c63a7fe59b495a78 SURFACE WATER
## 7  55942a58c63a7fe59b495a79 EARTH SCIENCE
```

```
## 8   55942a58c63a7fe59b495a79    HYDROSPHERE
## 9   55942a58c63a7fe59b495a79  SURFACE WATER
## 10  55942a58c63a7fe59b495a7a  EARTH SCIENCE
## # ... with 126,804 more rows
```

This is a tidy data frame because we have one row for each keyword; this means we will have multiple rows for each dataset because a dataset can have more than one keyword.

Now it is time to use tidytext's `unnest_tokens()` for the title and description fields so we can do the text analysis. Let's also remove stop words from the titles and descriptions. We will not remove stop words from the keywords, because those are short, human-assigned keywords like "RADIATION" or "CLIMATE INDICATORS."

```
library(tidytext)

nasa_title <- nasa_title %>%
  unnest_tokens(word, title) %>%
  anti_join(stop_words)

nasa_desc <- nasa_desc %>%
  unnest_tokens(word, desc) %>%
  anti_join(stop_words)
```

These are now in the tidy text format that we have been working with throughout this book, with one token (word, in this case) per row; let's take a look before we move on in our analysis.

```
nasa_title

## # A tibble: 210,914 × 2
##                               id          word
##                            <chr>         <chr>
## 1  56d07ee5a759fdadc44e5923        marble
## 2  56d07ee5a759fdadc44e5923          epic
## 3  56d07c16a759fdadc44e5922        fitara
## 4  56d07c16a759fdadc44e5922          ocio
## 5  56cf5b00a759fdadc44e5849  implementing
## 6  56cf5b00a759fdadc44e5846       receding
## 7  56cf5b00a759fdadc44e5846      recursive
## 8  56cf5b00a759fdadc44e5840     complaints
## 9  56cf5b00a759fdadc44e583b          score
## 10 56cf5b00a759fdadc44e583a            fix
## # ... with 210,904 more rows

nasa_desc

## # A tibble: 2,677,811 × 2
##                               id          word
##                            <chr>         <chr>
## 1  56d07c16a759fdadc44e5922        fitara
## 2  56d07c16a759fdadc44e5922          ocio
## 3  56cf5b00a759fdadc44e584a  degradation's
```

```
## 4   56cf5b00a759fdadc44e5847        dchwp1s
## 5   56cf5b00a759fdadc44e5847        dchwp1sp
## 6   56cf5b00a759fdadc44e5847         dchwdp
## 7   56cf5b00a759fdadc44e5847        dchwsnf
## 8   56cf5b00a759fdadc44e5847        dchwssf
## 9   56cf5b00a759fdadc44e5847        bursting
## 10  56cf5b00a759fdadc44e5847 consequentially
## # ... with 2,677,801 more rows
```

Some Initial Simple Exploration

What are the most common words in the NASA dataset titles? We can use `count()` from dplyr to check this out.

```
nasa_title %>%
  count(word, sort = TRUE)

## # A tibble: 11,614 × 2
##       word      n
##      <chr>  <int>
## 1  project   7735
## 2     data   3354
## 3        1   2841
## 4    level   2400
## 5   global   1809
## 6       v1   1478
## 7    daily   1397
## 8        3   1364
## 9     aura   1363
## 10      l2   1311
## # ... with 11,604 more rows
```

What about the descriptions?

```
nasa_desc %>%
  count(word, sort = TRUE)

## # A tibble: 35,940 × 2
##         word      n
##        <chr>  <int>
## 1       data  68871
## 2      modis  24420
## 3     global  23028
## 4          2  16599
## 5          1  15770
## 6     system  15480
## 7    product  14780
## 8       aqua  14738
## 9      earth  14373
## 10 resolution 13879
## # ... with 35,930 more rows
```

Words like "data" and "global" are used very often in NASA titles and descriptions. We may want to remove digits and some "words" like "v1" from these data frames for many types of analyses; they are not too meaningful for most audiences.

 We can do this by making a list of custom stop words and using anti_join() to remove them from the data frame, just like we removed the default stop words that are in the tidytext package. This approach can be used in many instances and is a great tool to bear in mind.

```
my_stopwords <- data_frame(word = c(as.character(1:10),
                                    "v1", "v03", "l2", "l3", "l4", "v5.2.0",
                                    "v003", "v004", "v005", "v006", "v7"))
nasa_title <- nasa_title %>%
  anti_join(my_stopwords)
nasa_desc <- nasa_desc %>%
  anti_join(my_stopwords)
```

What are the most common keywords?

```
nasa_keyword %>%
  group_by(keyword) %>%
  count(sort = TRUE)

## # A tibble: 1,774 × 2
##                     keyword     n
##                       <chr> <int>
## 1             EARTH SCIENCE 14362
## 2                   Project  7452
## 3                ATMOSPHERE  7321
## 4               Ocean Color  7268
## 5              Ocean Optics  7268
## 6                    Oceans  7268
## 7                 completed  6452
## 8     ATMOSPHERIC WATER VAPOR 3142
## 9                    OCEANS  2765
## 10             LAND SURFACE  2720
## # ... with 1,764 more rows
```

We likely want to change all of the keywords to either lower- or uppercase to get rid of duplicates like "OCEANS" and "Oceans." Let's do that here.

```
nasa_keyword <- nasa_keyword %>%
  mutate(keyword = toupper(keyword))
```

Word Co-ocurrences and Correlations

As a next step, let's examine which words commonly occur together in the titles, descriptions, and keywords of NASA datasets, as described in Chapter 4. We can then examine word networks for these fields; this may help us see, for example, which datasets are related to each other.

Networks of Description and Title Words

We can use `pairwise_count()` from the widyr package to count how many times each pair of words occurs together in a title or description field.

```
library(widyr)

title_word_pairs <- nasa_title %>%
  pairwise_count(word, id, sort = TRUE, upper = FALSE)

title_word_pairs
```

```
## # A tibble: 156,689 × 3
##       item1   item2     n
##       <chr>   <chr> <dbl>
## 1   system project   796
## 2      lba     eco   683
## 3     airs    aqua   641
## 4    level    aqua   623
## 5    level    airs   612
## 6     aura     omi   607
## 7   global    grid   597
## 8   global   daily   574
## 9     data  boreas   551
## 10  ground     gpm   550
## # ... with 156,679 more rows
```

These are the pairs of words that occur together most often in title fields. Some of these words are obviously acronyms used within NASA, and we see how often words like "project" and "system" are used.

```
desc_word_pairs <- nasa_desc %>%
  pairwise_count(word, id, sort = TRUE, upper = FALSE)

desc_word_pairs
```

```
## # A tibble: 10,889,084 × 3
##          item1      item2     n
##          <chr>      <chr> <dbl>
## 1         data     global  9864
## 2         data resolution  9302
## 3   instrument resolution  8189
## 4         data    surface  8180
## 5       global resolution  8139
## 6         data instrument  7994
## 7         data     system  7870
## 8   resolution      bands  7584
## 9         data      earth  7576
```

```
## 10        orbit resolution  7462
## # ... with 10,889,074 more rows
```

These are the pairs of words that occur together most often in descripton fields. "Data" is a very common word in description fields; there is no shortage of data in the datasets at NASA!

Let's plot networks of these co-occurring words so we can see these relationships better in Figure 8-1. We will again use the ggraph package for visualizing our networks.

```
library(ggplot2)
library(igraph)
library(ggraph)

set.seed(1234)
title_word_pairs %>%
  filter(n >= 250) %>%
  graph_from_data_frame() %>%
  ggraph(layout = "fr") +
  geom_edge_link(aes(edge_alpha = n, edge_width = n), edge_colour = "cyan4") +
  geom_node_point(size = 5) +
  geom_node_text(aes(label = name), repel = TRUE,
                 point.padding = unit(0.2, "lines")) +
  theme_void()
```

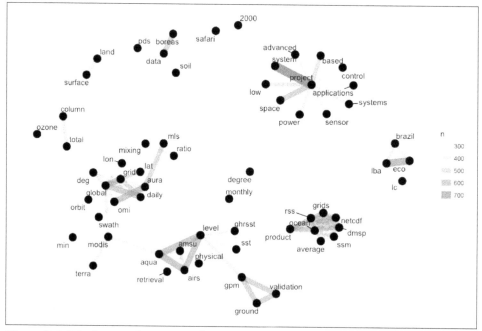

Figure 8-1. Word network in NASA dataset titles

We see some clear clustering in this network of title words; words in NASA dataset titles are largely organized into several families of words that tend to go together.

What about the words from the description fields (Figure 8-2)?

```
set.seed(1234)
desc_word_pairs %>%
  filter(n >= 5000) %>%
  graph_from_data_frame() %>%
  ggraph(layout = "fr") +
  geom_edge_link(aes(edge_alpha = n, edge_width = n), edge_colour = "darkred") +
  geom_node_point(size = 5) +
  geom_node_text(aes(label = name), repel = TRUE,
                 point.padding = unit(0.2, "lines")) +
  theme_void()
```

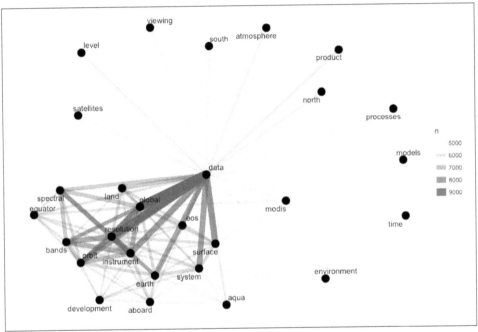

Figure 8-2. Word network in NASA dataset descriptions

Figure 8-2 shows such *strong* connections between the top dozen or so words (words like "data," "global," "resolution," and "instrument") that we do not see a clear clustering structure in the network. We may want to use tf-idf (as described in detail in Chapter 3) as a metric to find characteristic words for each description field, instead of looking at counts of words.

Networks of Keywords

Next, let's make a network of the keywords in Figure 8-3 to see which keywords commonly occur together in the same datasets.

```
keyword_pairs <- nasa_keyword %>%
  pairwise_count(keyword, id, sort = TRUE, upper = FALSE)

keyword_pairs

## # A tibble: 13,390 × 3
##              item1                       item2     n
##              <chr>                       <chr> <dbl>
## 1           OCEANS              OCEAN OPTICS  7324
## 2    EARTH SCIENCE                ATMOSPHERE  7318
## 3           OCEANS               OCEAN COLOR  7270
## 4     OCEAN OPTICS               OCEAN COLOR  7270
## 5          PROJECT                 COMPLETED  6450
## 6    EARTH SCIENCE ATMOSPHERIC WATER VAPOR  3142
## 7       ATMOSPHERE ATMOSPHERIC WATER VAPOR  3142
## 8    EARTH SCIENCE                    OCEANS  2762
## 9    EARTH SCIENCE              LAND SURFACE  2718
## 10   EARTH SCIENCE                 BIOSPHERE  2448
## # ... with 13,380 more rows

set.seed(1234)
keyword_pairs %>%
  filter(n >= 700) %>%
  graph_from_data_frame() %>%
  ggraph(layout = "fr") +
  geom_edge_link(aes(edge_alpha = n, edge_width = n),
                 edge_colour = "royalblue") +
  geom_node_point(size = 5) +
  geom_node_text(aes(label = name), repel = TRUE,
                 point.padding = unit(0.2, "lines")) +
  theme_void()
```

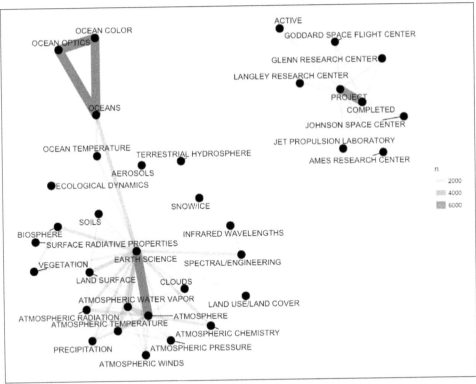

Figure 8-3. Co-occurrence network in NASA dataset keywords

We definitely see clustering here, and strong connections between keywords like "OCEANS," "OCEAN OPTICS," and "OCEAN COLOR," or "PROJECT" and "COMPLETED."

These are the most commonly co-occurring words, but also just the most common keywords in general.

To examine the relationships among keywords in a different way, we can find the correlation among the keywords as described in Chapter 4. This looks for those keywords that are more likely to occur together than with other keywords in a description field.

```
keyword_cors <- nasa_keyword %>%
  group_by(keyword) %>%
  filter(n() >= 50) %>%
  pairwise_cor(keyword, id, sort = TRUE, upper = FALSE)
```

```
keyword_cors

## # A tibble: 7,875 × 3
##                       item1        item2 correlation
##                       <chr>        <chr>       <dbl>
## 1                 KNOWLEDGE      SHARING   1.0000000
## 2                  DASHLINK         AMES   1.0000000
## 3                  SCHEDULE    EXPEDITION  1.0000000
## 4                 TURBULENCE       MODELS  0.9971871
## 5                     APPEL    KNOWLEDGE   0.9967945
## 6                     APPEL      SHARING   0.9967945
## 7               OCEAN OPTICS  OCEAN COLOR  0.9952123
## 8       ATMOSPHERIC SCIENCE        CLOUD  0.9938681
## 9                    LAUNCH     SCHEDULE  0.9837078
## 10                   LAUNCH    EXPEDITION  0.9837078
## # ... with 7,865 more rows
```

Notice that these keywords at the top of this sorted data frame have correlation coefficients equal to 1; they always occur together. This means these are redundant keywords. It may not make sense to continue to use both of the keywords in these sets of pairs; instead, just one keyword could be used.

Let's visualize the network of keyword correlations, just as we did for keyword co-occurences (Figure 8-4).

```
set.seed(1234)
keyword_cors %>%
  filter(correlation > .6) %>%
  graph_from_data_frame() %>%
  ggraph(layout = "fr") +
  geom_edge_link(aes(edge_alpha = correlation, edge_width = correlation),
                 edge_colour = "royalblue") +
  geom_node_point(size = 5) +
  geom_node_text(aes(label = name), repel = TRUE,
                 point.padding = unit(0.2, "lines")) +
  theme_void()
```

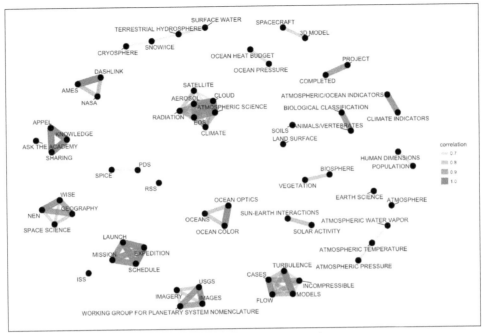

Figure 8-4. Correlation network in NASA dataset keywords

This network in Figure 8-4 appears much different than the co-occurence network. The difference is that the co-occurrence network asks a question about which keyword pairs occur most often, and the correlation network asks a question about which keywords occur more often together than with other keywords. Notice here the high number of small clusters of keywords; the network structure can be extracted (for further analysis) from the `graph_from_data_frame()` function above.

Calculating tf-idf for the Description Fields

The network graph in Figure 8-2 showed us that the description fields are dominated by a few common words like "data," "global," and "resolution"; this would be an excellent opportunity to use tf-idf as a statistic to find characteristic words for individual description fields. As discussed in Chapter 3, we can use tf-idf, the term frequency times inverse document frequency, to identify words that are especially important to a document within a collection of documents. Let's apply that approach to the description fields of these NASA datasets.

What Is tf-idf for the Description Field Words?

We will consider each description field a document, and the whole set of description fields the collection or corpus of documents. We have already used `unnest_tokens()`

earlier in this chapter to make a tidy data frame of the words in the description fields, so now we can use `bind_tf_idf()` to calculate tf-idf for each word.

```
desc_tf_idf <- nasa_desc %>%
  count(id, word, sort = TRUE) %>%
  ungroup() %>%
  bind_tf_idf(word, id, n)
```

What are the highest tf-idf words in the NASA description fields?

```
desc_tf_idf %>%
  arrange(-tf_idf) %>%
  select(-id)
```

```
## # A tibble: 1,913,224 × 6
##                                                  word     n    tf        idf
##                                                 <chr> <int> <dbl>      <dbl>
## 1                                                 rdr     1     1 10.375052
## 2      palsar_radiometric_terrain_corrected_high_res     1     1 10.375052
## 3      cpalsar_radiometric_terrain_corrected_low_res     1     1 10.375052
## 4                                                lgrs     1     1  8.765615
## 5                                                lgrs     1     1  8.765615
## 6                                                lgrs     1     1  8.765615
## 7                                                 mri     1     1  8.583293
## 8                              template_proddescription     1     1  8.295611
## 9                              template_proddescription     1     1  8.295611
## 10                             template_proddescription     1     1  8.295611
## # ... with 1,913,214 more rows, and 1 more variables: tf_idf <dbl>
```

These are the most important words in the description fields as measured by tf-idf, meaning they are common but not too common.

 Notice we have run into an issue here; both n and term frequency are equal to 1 for these terms, meaning that these were description fields that only had a single word in them. If a description field only contains one word, the tf-idf algorithm will think that is a very important word.

Depending on our analytic goals, it might be a good idea to throw out all description fields that have very few words.

Connecting Description Fields to Keywords

We now know which words in the descriptions have high tf-idf, and we also have labels for these descriptions in the keywords. Let's do a full join of the keyword data frame and the data frame of description words with tf-idf, and then find the highest tf-idf words for a given keyword.

```
desc_tf_idf <- full_join(desc_tf_idf, nasa_keyword, by = "id")
```

Let's plot some of the most important words, as measured by tf-idf, for a few example keywords used on NASA datasets. First, let's use dplyr operations to filter for the keywords we want to examine and take just the top 15 words for each keyword. Then, let's plot those words in Figure 8-5.

```
desc_tf_idf %>%
  filter(!near(tf, 1)) %>%
  filter(keyword %in% c("SOLAR ACTIVITY", "CLOUDS",
                        "SEISMOLOGY", "ASTROPHYSICS",
                        "HUMAN HEALTH", "BUDGET")) %>%
  arrange(desc(tf_idf)) %>%
  group_by(keyword) %>%
  distinct(word, keyword, .keep_all = TRUE) %>%
  top_n(15, tf_idf) %>%
  ungroup() %>%
  mutate(word = factor(word, levels = rev(unique(word)))) %>%
  ggplot(aes(word, tf_idf, fill = keyword)) +
  geom_col(show.legend = FALSE) +
  facet_wrap(~keyword, ncol = 3, scales = "free") +
  coord_flip() +
  labs(title = "Highest tf-idf words in NASA metadata description fields",
       caption = "NASA metadata from https://data.nasa.gov/data.json",
       x = NULL, y = "tf-idf")
```

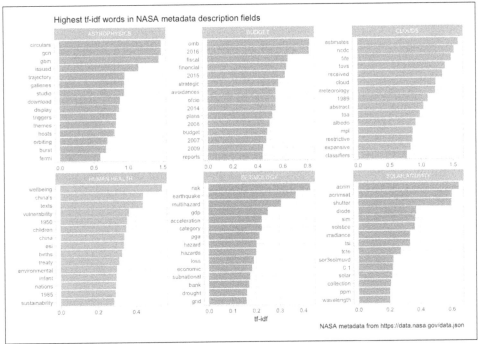

Figure 8-5. Distribution of tf-idf for words from datasets labeled with select keywords

Using tf-idf has allowed us to identify important description words for each of these keywords. Datasets labeled with the keyword "SEISMOLOGY" have words like "earthquake," "risk," and "hazard" in their description, while those labeled with "HUMAN HEALTH" have descriptions characterized by words like "wellbeing," "vulnerability," and "children." Most of the combinations of letters that are not English words are certainly acronyms (like OMB for the Office of Management and Budget), and the examples of years and numbers are important for these topics. The tf-idf statistic has identified the kinds of words it is intended to—important words for individual documents within a collection of documents.

Topic Modeling

Using tf-idf as a statistic has already given us insight into the content of NASA description fields, but let's try an additional approach to the question of what the NASA descriptions fields are about. We can use topic modeling, as described in Chapter 6, to model each document (description field) as a mixture of topics, and each topic as a mixture of words. As in earlier chapters, we will use latent Dirichlet allocation (LDA) (*https://en.wikipedia.org/wiki/Latent_Dirichlet_allocation*) for our topic modeling; there are other possible approaches for topic modeling.

Casting to a Document-Term Matrix

To do the topic modeling as implemented here, we need to make a `DocumentTermMa trix`, a special kind of matrix from the tm package (of course, this is just a specific implementation of the general concept of a "document-term matrix"). Rows correspond to documents (description texts in our case), and columns correspond to terms (i.e., words); it is a sparse matrix and the values are word counts.

Let's clean up the text a bit using stop words to remove some of the nonsense "words" left over from HTML or other character encoding. We can use `bind_rows()` to add our custom stop words to the list of default stop words from the tidytext package, and then use `anti_join()` to remove them all at once from our data frame.

```
my_stop_words <- bind_rows(stop_words,
                    data_frame(word = c("nbsp", "amp", "gt", "lt",
                                        "timesnewromanpsmt", "font",
                                        "td", "li", "br", "tr", "quot",
                                        "st", "img", "src", "strong",
                                        "http", "file", "files",
                                        as.character(1:12)),
                        lexicon = rep("custom", 30)))

word_counts <- nasa_desc %>%
  anti_join(my_stop_words) %>%
  count(id, word, sort = TRUE) %>%
  ungroup()
```

```
word_counts

## # A tibble: 1,895,310 × 3
##                              id     word       n
##                           <chr>    <chr>   <int>
## 1  55942a8ec63a7fe59b4986ef      suit      82
## 2  55942a8ec63a7fe59b4986ef     space      69
## 3  56cf5b00a759fdadc44e564a      data      41
## 4  56cf5b00a759fdadc44e564a      leak      40
## 5  56cf5b00a759fdadc44e564a      tree      39
## 6  55942a8ec63a7fe59b4986ef  pressure      34
## 7  55942a8ec63a7fe59b4986ef    system      34
## 8  55942a89c63a7fe59b4982d9        em      32
## 9  55942a8ec63a7fe59b4986ef        al      32
## 10 55942a8ec63a7fe59b4986ef     human      31
## # ... with 1,895,300 more rows
```

This is the information we need, the number of times each word is used in each document, to make a DocumentTermMatrix. We can cast() from our tidy text format to this nontidy format, as described in detail in Chapter 5.

```
desc_dtm <- word_counts %>%
  cast_dtm(id, word, n)

desc_dtm

## <<DocumentTermMatrix (documents: 32003, terms: 35901)>>
## Non-/sparse entries: 1895310/1147044393
## Sparsity           : 100%
## Maximal term length: 166
## Weighting          : term frequency (tf)
```

We see that this dataset contains documents (each of them a NASA description field) and terms (words). Notice that this example document-term matrix is (very close to) 100% sparse, meaning that almost all of the entries in this matrix are zero. Each nonzero entry corresponds to a certain word appearing in a certain document.

Ready for Topic Modeling

Now let's use the topicmodels (*https://cran.r-project.org/package=topicmodels*) package to create an LDA model. How many topics will we tell the algorithm to make? This is a question much like in k-means clustering; we don't really know ahead of time. We tried the following modeling procedure using 8, 16, 24, 32, and 64 topics; we found that at 24 topics, documents are still getting sorted into topics cleanly, but going much beyond that caused the distributions of γ, the probability that each document belongs in each topic, to look worrisome. We will show more details on this later.

```
library(topicmodels)

# be aware that running this model is time intensive
desc_lda <- LDA(desc_dtm, k = 24, control = list(seed = 1234))
desc_lda

## A LDA_VEM topic model with 24 topics.
```

This is a stochastic algorithm that could have different results depending on where the algorithm starts, so we need to specify a seed for reproducibility as shown here.

Interpreting the Topic Model

Now that we have built the model, let's tidy() the results of the model, i.e., construct a tidy data frame that summarizes the results of the model. The tidytext package includes a tidying method for LDA models from the topicmodels package.

```
tidy_lda <- tidy(desc_lda)

tidy_lda

## # A tibble: 861,624 × 3
##     topic  term          beta
##     <int> <chr>         <dbl>
## 1      1   suit 1.003981e-121
## 2      2   suit 2.630614e-145
## 3      3   suit  1.916240e-79
## 4      4   suit  6.715725e-45
## 5      5   suit  1.738334e-85
## 6      6   suit  7.692116e-84
## 7      7   suit  3.283851e-04
## 8      8   suit  3.738586e-20
## 9      9   suit  4.846953e-15
## 10    10   suit  4.765471e-10
## # ... with 861,614 more rows
```

The column β tells us the probability of that term being generated from that topic for that document. It is the probability of that term (word) belonging to that topic. Notice that some of the values for β are very, very low, and some are not so low.

What is each topic about? Let's examine the top 10 terms for each topic.

```
top_terms <- tidy_lda %>%
  group_by(topic) %>%
  top_n(10, beta) %>%
  ungroup() %>%
  arrange(topic, -beta)

top_terms

## # A tibble: 240 × 3
##     topic        term       beta
##     <int>       <chr>      <dbl>
```

```
## 1      1        data 0.04488960
## 2      1        soil 0.03676198
## 3      1    moisture 0.02954555
## 4      1        amsr 0.02437751
## 5      1         sst 0.01684001
## 6      1  validation 0.01322457
## 7      1 temperature 0.01317075
## 8      1     surface 0.01290046
## 9      1    accuracy 0.01225131
## 10     1         set 0.01155372
## # ... with 230 more rows
```

It is not very easy to interpret what the topics are about from a data frame like this, so let's look at this information visually in Figures 8-6 and 8-7.

```
top_terms %>%
  mutate(term = reorder(term, beta)) %>%
  group_by(topic, term) %>%
  arrange(desc(beta)) %>%
  ungroup() %>%
  mutate(term = factor(paste(term, topic, sep = "__"),
                       levels = rev(paste(term, topic, sep = "__")))) %>%
  ggplot(aes(term, beta, fill = as.factor(topic))) +
  geom_col(show.legend = FALSE) +
  coord_flip() +
  scale_x_discrete(labels = function(x) gsub("__.+$", "", x)) +
  labs(title = "Top 10 terms in each LDA topic",
       x = NULL, y = expression(beta)) +
  facet_wrap(~ topic, ncol = 3, scales = "free")
```

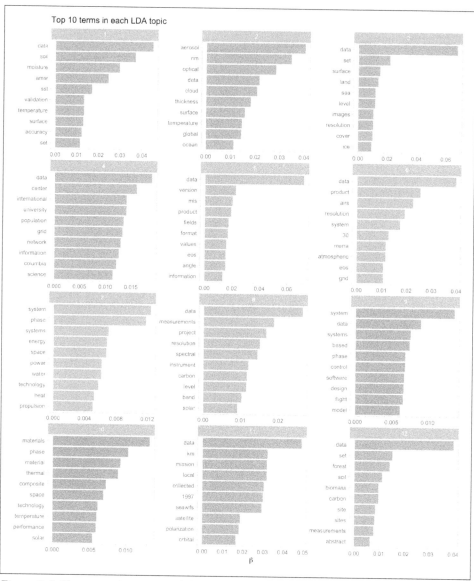

Figure 8-6. Top terms in topic modeling of NASA metadata description field texts

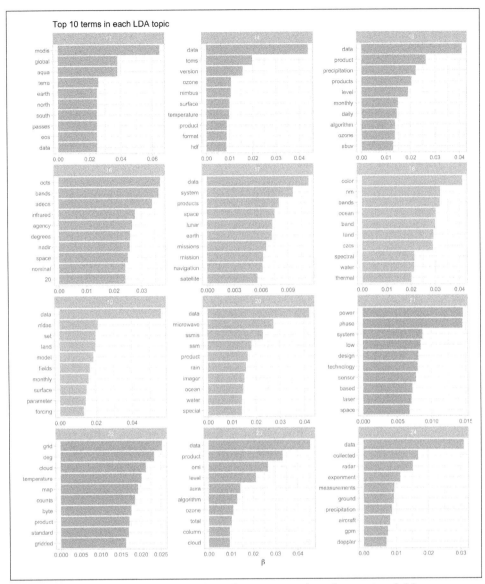

Figure 8-7. Top terms in topic modeling of NASA metadata description field texts

We can see what a dominant word "data" is in these description texts. In addition, there are meaningful differences between these collections of terms, from terms about soil, forests, and biomass in topic 12 to terms about design, systems, and technology in topic 21. The topic modeling process has identified groupings of terms that we can understand as human readers of these description fields.

We just explored which words are associated with which topics. Next, let's examine which topics are associated with which description fields (i.e., documents). We will look at a different probability for this, γ, the probability that each document belongs in each topic, again using the tidy verb.

```
lda_gamma <- tidy(desc_lda, matrix = "gamma")

lda_gamma

## # A tibble: 768,072 × 3
##                      document topic       gamma
##                         <chr> <int>       <dbl>
## 1   55942a8ec63a7fe59b4986ef     1 6.453820e-06
## 2   56cf5b00a759fdadc44e564a     1 1.158393e-05
## 3   55942a89c63a7fe59b4982d9     1 4.917441e-02
## 4   56cf5b00a759fdadc44e55cd     1 2.249043e-05
## 5   55942a89c63a7fe59b4982c6     1 6.609442e-05
## 6   55942a86c63a7fe59b498077     1 5.666520e-05
## 7   56cf5b00a759fdadc44e56f8     1 4.752082e-05
## 8   55942a8bc63a7fe59b4984b5     1 4.308534e-05
## 9   55942a6ec63a7fe59b496bf7     1 4.408626e-05
## 10  55942a8ec63a7fe59b4986f6     1 2.878188e-05
## # ... with 768,062 more rows
```

Notice that some of the probabilities visible at the top of the data frame are low and some are higher. Our model has assigned a probability to each description belonging to each of the topics we constructed from the sets of words. How are the probabilities distributed? Let's visualize them (Figure 8-8).

```
ggplot(lda_gamma, aes(gamma)) +
  geom_histogram() +
  scale_y_log10() +
  labs(title = "Distribution of probabilities for all topics",
       y = "Number of documents", x = expression(gamma))
```

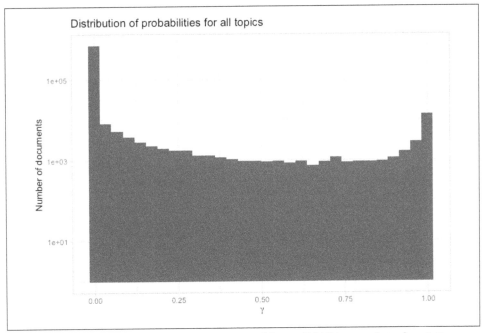

Figure 8-8. Probability distribution in topic modeling of NASA metadata description field texts

First notice that the y-axis is plotted on a log scale; otherwise it is difficult to make out any detail in the plot. Next, notice that γ runs from 0 to 1; remember that this is the probability that a given document belongs in a given topic. There are many values near zero, which means there are many documents that do not belong in each topic. Also, there are many values near $\gamma = 1$; these are the documents that *do* belong in those topics. This distribution shows that documents are being well discriminated as belonging to a topic or not. We can also look at how the probabilities are distributed within each topic, as shown in Figure 8-9.

```
ggplot(lda_gamma, aes(gamma, fill = as.factor(topic))) +
  geom_histogram(show.legend = FALSE) +
  facet_wrap(~ topic, ncol = 4) +
  scale_y_log10() +
  labs(title = "Distribution of probability for each topic",
       y = "Number of documents", x = expression(gamma))
```

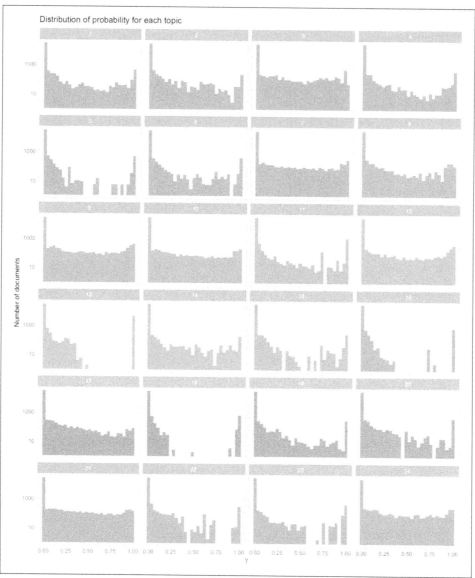

Figure 8-9. Probability distribution for each topic in topic modeling of NASA metadata description field texts

Let's look specifically at topic 18 in Figure 8-9, a topic that had documents cleanly sorted in and out of it. There are many documents with γ close to 1; these are the documents that *do* belong to topic 18 according to the model. There are also many documents with γ close to 0; these are the documents that do *not* belong to topic 18.

Each document appears in each panel in this plot, and its γ for that topic tells us that document's probability of belonging in that topic.

This plot displays the type of information we used to choose the number of topics for our topic modeling procedure. When we tried options higher than 24 (such as 32 or 64), the distributions for γ started to look very flat toward $\gamma = 1$; documents were not getting sorted into topics very well.

Connecting Topic Modeling with Keywords

Let's connect these topic models with the keywords and see what relationships we can find. We can full_join() this to the human-tagged keywords and discover which keywords are associated with which topic.

```
lda_gamma <- full_join(lda_gamma, nasa_keyword, by = c("document" = "id"))

lda_gamma
```

```
## # A tibble: 3,037,671 × 4
##                    document topic        gamma                     keyword
##                       <chr> <int>        <dbl>                       <chr>
## 1  55942a8ec63a7fe59b4986ef     1 6.453820e-06        JOHNSON SPACE CENTER
## 2  55942a8ec63a7fe59b4986ef     1 6.453820e-06                     PROJECT
## 3  55942a8ec63a7fe59b4986ef     1 6.453820e-06                   COMPLETED
## 4  56cf5b00a759fdadc44e564a     1 1.158393e-05                    DASHLINK
## 5  56cf5b00a759fdadc44e564a     1 1.158393e-05                        AMES
## 6  56cf5b00a759fdadc44e564a     1 1.158393e-05                        NASA
## 7  55942a89c63a7fe59b4982d9     1 4.917441e-02 GODDARD SPACE FLIGHT CENTER
## 8  55942a89c63a7fe59b4982d9     1 4.917441e-02                     PROJECT
## 9  55942a89c63a7fe59b4982d9     1 4.917441e-02                   COMPLETED
## 10 56cf5b00a759fdadc44e55cd     1 2.249043e-05                    DASHLINK
## # ... with 3,037,661 more rows
```

Now we can use filter() to keep only the document-topic entries that have probabilities (γ) greater than some cutoff value; let's use 0.9.

```
top_keywords <- lda_gamma %>%
  filter(gamma > 0.9) %>%
  count(topic, keyword, sort = TRUE)

top_keywords
```

```
## Source: local data frame [1,022 × 3]
## Groups: topic [24]
##
##    topic       keyword     n
##    <int>         <chr> <int>
## 1     13   OCEAN COLOR  4480
## 2     13   OCEAN OPTICS  4480
## 3     13        OCEANS  4480
## 4     11   OCEAN COLOR  1216
## 5     11   OCEAN OPTICS  1216
```

```
## 6       11         OCEANS  1216
## 7        9        PROJECT   926
## 8       12  EARTH SCIENCE   909
## 9        9      COMPLETED   834
## 10      16    OCEAN COLOR   768
## # ... with 1,012 more rows
```

What are the top keywords for each topic (Figure 8-10)?

```
top_keywords %>%
  group_by(topic) %>%
  top_n(5, n) %>%
  group_by(topic, keyword) %>%
  arrange(desc(n)) %>%
  ungroup() %>%
  mutate(keyword = factor(paste(keyword, topic, sep = "__"),
                          levels = rev(paste(keyword, topic, sep = "__")))) %>%
  ggplot(aes(keyword, n, fill = as.factor(topic))) +
  geom_col(show.legend = FALSE) +
  labs(title = "Top keywords for each LDA topic",
       x = NULL, y = "Number of documents") +
  coord_flip() +
  scale_x_discrete(labels = function(x) gsub("__.+$", "", x)) +
  facet_wrap(~ topic, ncol = 3, scales = "free")
```

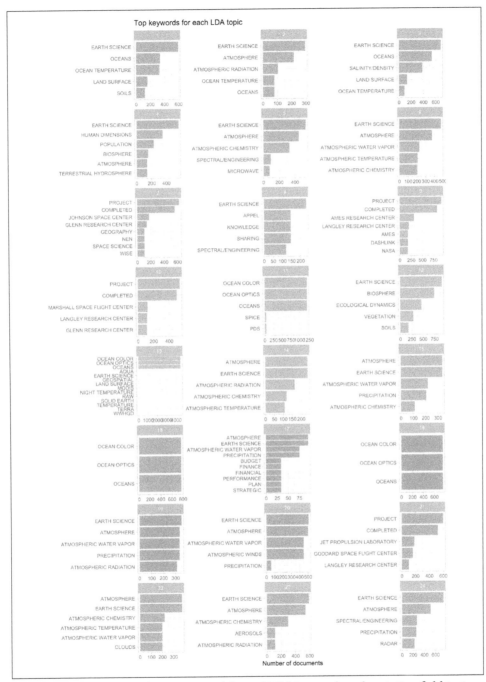

Figure 8-10. Top keywords in topic modeling of NASA metadata description field texts

Let's take a step back and remind ourselves what Figure 8-10 is telling us. NASA datasets are tagged with keywords by human beings, and we have built an LDA topic model (with 24 topics) for the description fields of the NASA datasets. This plot answers the question, "For the datasets with description fields that have a high probability of belonging to a given topic, what are the most common human-assigned keywords?"

It's interesting that the keywords for topics 13, 16, and 18 are essentially duplicates of each other ("OCEAN COLOR," "OCEAN OPTICS," "OCEANS"), because the top words in those topics do exhibit meaningful differences, as shown in Figures 8-6 and 8-7. Also note that by number of documents, the combination of 13, 16, and 18 is quite a large percentage of the total number of datasets represented in this plot, and even more if we were to include topic 11. By number, there are *many* datasets at NASA that deal with oceans, ocean color, and ocean optics. We see "PROJECT COMPLETED" in topics 9, 10, and 21, along with the names of NASA laboratories and research centers. Other important subject areas that stand out are groups of keywords about atmospheric science, budget/finance, and population/human dimensions. We can go back to Figures 8-6 and 8-7 on terms and topics to see which words in the description fields are driving datasets being assigned to these topics. For example, topic 4 is associated with keywords about population and human dimensions, and some of the top terms for that topic are "population," "international," "center," and "university."

Summary

By using a combination of network analysis, tf-idf, and topic modeling, we have come to a greater understanding of how datasets are related at NASA. Specifically, we have more information now about how keywords are connected to each other and which datasets are likely to be related. The topic model could be used to suggest keywords based on the words in the description field, or the work on the keywords could suggest the most important combination of keywords for certain areas of study.

## CHAPTER 9

Case Study: Analyzing Usenet Text

In our final chapter, we'll use what we've learned in this book to perform a start-to-finish analysis of a set of 20,000 messages sent to 20 Usenet bulletin boards in 1993. The Usenet bulletin boards in this dataset include newsgroups for topics like politics, religion, cars, sports, and cryptography, and offer a rich set of text written by many users. This data set is publicly available at *http://qwone.com/~jason/20Newsgroups/* (the *20news-bydate.tar.gz* file) and has become popular for exercises in text analysis and machine learning.

Preprocessing

We'll start by reading in all the messages from the *20news-bydate* folder, which are organized in subfolders with one file for each message. We can read in files like these with a combination of read_lines(), map(), and unnest().

> Note that this step may take several minutes to read all the documents.

```
library(dplyr)
library(tidyr)
library(purrr)
library(readr)

training_folder <- "data/20news-bydate/20news-bydate-train/"

# Define a function to read all files from a folder into a data frame
read_folder <- function(infolder) {
  data_frame(file = dir(infolder, full.names = TRUE)) %>%
```

```
    mutate(text = map(file, read_lines)) %>%
    transmute(id = basename(file), text) %>%
    unnest(text)
}

# Use unnest() and map() to apply read_folder to each subfolder
raw_text <- data_frame(folder = dir(training_folder, full.names = TRUE)) %>%
  unnest(map(folder, read_folder)) %>%
  transmute(newsgroup = basename(folder), id, text)

raw_text

# A tibble: 511,655 x 3
      newsgroup     id
         <chr> <chr>
 1 alt.atheism 49960
 2 alt.atheism 49960
 3 alt.atheism 49960
 4 alt.atheism 49960
 5 alt.atheism 49960
 6 alt.atheism 49960
 7 alt.atheism 49960
 8 alt.atheism 49960
 9 alt.atheism 49960
10 alt.atheism 49960
# ... with 511,645 more rows, and 1 more variables: text <chr>
```

Notice the newsgroup column, which describes which of the 20 newsgroups each message comes from, and the id column, which identifies a unique message within that newsgroup. What newsgroups are included, and how many messages were posted in each (Figure 9-1)?

```
library(ggplot2)

raw_text %>%
  group_by(newsgroup) %>%
  summarize(messages = n_distinct(id)) %>%
  ggplot(aes(newsgroup, messages)) +
  geom_col() +
  coord_flip()
```

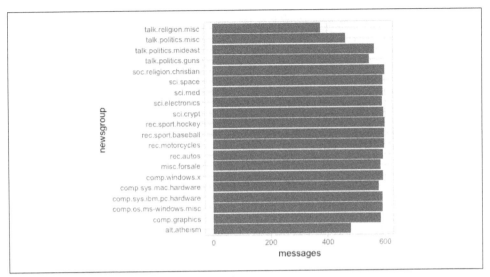

Figure 9-1. Number of messages from each newsgroup

We can see that Usenet newsgroup names are named hierarchically, starting with a main topic such as "talk," "sci," or "rec," followed by further specifications.

Preprocessing Text

Most of the datasets we've examined in this book were preprocessed, meaning we didn't have to remove, for example, copyright notices from the Jane Austen novels. Here, however, each message has some structure and extra text that we don't want to include in our analysis. For example, every message has a header containing fields such as "from:" or "in_reply_to:" that describe the message. Some also have automated email signatures, which occur after a line like --.

This kind of preprocessing can be done within the dplyr package, using a combination of cumsum() (cumulative sum) and str_detect() from stringr.

```
library(stringr)

# must occur after the first occurrence of an empty line,
# and before the first occurrence of a line starting with --
cleaned_text <- raw_text %>%
  group_by(newsgroup, id) %>%
  filter(cumsum(text == "") > 0,
         cumsum(str_detect(text, "^--")) == 0) %>%
  ungroup()
```

Many lines also have nested text representing quotes from other users, typically starting with a line like "so-and-so writes…" These can be removed with a few regular expressions.

We also choose to manually remove two messages, 9704 and 9985, that contain a large amount of nontext content.

```
cleaned_text <- cleaned_text %>%
  filter(str_detect(text, "^[^>]+[A-Za-z\\d]") | text == "",
         !str_detect(text, "writes(:|\\.\\.\\.\\.)$"),
         !str_detect(text, "^In article <"),
         !id %in% c(9704, 9985))
```

At this point, we're ready to use `unnest_tokens()` to split the dataset into tokens, while removing stop words.

```
library(tidytext)

usenet_words <- cleaned_text %>%
  unnest_tokens(word, text) %>%
  filter(str_detect(word, "[a-z']$"),
         !word %in% stop_words$word)
```

Every raw text dataset will require different steps for data cleaning, which will often involve some trial and error, and exploration of unusual cases in the dataset. It's important to notice that this cleaning can be achieved using tidy tools such as dplyr and tidyr.

Words in Newsgroups

Now that we've removed the headers, signatures, and formatting, we can start exploring common words. For starters, we could find the most common words in the entire dataset or within particular newsgroups.

```
usenet_words %>%
  count(word, sort = TRUE)

## # A tibble: 68,137 × 2
##             word     n
##            <chr> <int>
## 1         people  3655
## 2           time  2705
## 3            god  1626
## 4         system  1595
## 5        program  1103
## 6            bit  1097
## 7    information  1094
## 8        windows  1088
## 9     government  1084
## 10         space  1072
## # ... with 68,127 more rows
```

```
words_by_newsgroup <- usenet_words %>%
  count(newsgroup, word, sort = TRUE) %>%
  ungroup()

words_by_newsgroup
```

```
## # A tibble: 173,913 × 3
##                   newsgroup       word     n
##                       <chr>      <chr> <int>
## 1    soc.religion.christian        god   917
## 2                 sci.space      space   840
## 3      talk.politics.mideast     people   728
## 4                  sci.crypt        key   704
## 5   comp.os.ms-windows.misc    windows   625
## 6      talk.politics.mideast   armenian   582
## 7                  sci.crypt         db   549
## 8      talk.politics.mideast    turkish   514
## 9                  rec.autos        car   509
## 10     talk.politics.mideast  armenians   509
## # ... with 173,903 more rows
```

Finding tf-idf Within Newsgroups

We'd expect the newsgroups to differ in terms of topic and content, and therefore for the frequency of words to differ between them. Let's try quantifying this using the tf-idf metric (Chapter 3).

```
tf_idf <- words_by_newsgroup %>%
  bind_tf_idf(word, newsgroup, n) %>%
  arrange(desc(tf_idf))

tf_idf
```

```
# A tibble: 173,913 x 6
                     newsgroup          word     n         tf      idf
                         <chr>         <chr> <int>      <dbl>    <dbl>
1    comp.sys.ibm.pc.hardware          scsi   483 0.01761681 1.20397
2        talk.politics.mideast      armenian   582 0.00804890 2.30259
3               rec.motorcycles          bike   324 0.01389842 1.20397
4        talk.politics.mideast     armenians   509 0.00703933 2.30259
5                    sci.crypt    encryption   410 0.00816099 1.89712
6             rec.sport.hockey           nhl   157 0.00439665 2.99573
7          talk.politics.misc stephanopoulos   158 0.00416228 2.99573
8               rec.motorcycles         bikes    97 0.00416095 2.99573
9             rec.sport.hockey        hockey   270 0.00756112 1.60944
10               comp.windows.x         oname   136 0.00353550 2.99573
# ... with 173,903 more rows, and 1 more variables: tf_idf <dbl>
```

We can examine the top tf-idf for a few selected groups to extract words specific to those topics. For example, we could look at all the sci. boards, visualized in Figure 9-2.

```
tf_idf %>%
  filter(str_detect(newsgroup, "^sci\\.")) %>%
  group_by(newsgroup) %>%
  top_n(12, tf_idf) %>%
  ungroup() %>%
  mutate(word = reorder(word, tf_idf)) %>%
  ggplot(aes(word, tf_idf, fill = newsgroup)) +
  geom_col(show.legend = FALSE) +
  facet_wrap(~ newsgroup, scales = "free") +
  ylab("tf-idf") +
  coord_flip()
```

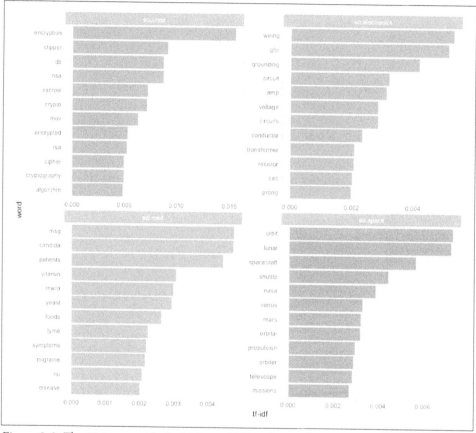

Figure 9-2. The 12 terms with the highest tf-idf within each of the science-related news-groups

We see lots of characteristic words specific to a particular newsgroup, such as "wiring" and "circuit" on the sci.electronics topic, and "orbit" and "lunar" for the space newsgroup. You could use this same code to explore other newsgroups yourself.

What newsgroups tend to be similar to each other in text content? We could discover this by finding the pairwise correlation of word frequencies within each newsgroup, using the `pairwise_cor()` function from the widyr package (see "Examining Pairwise Correlation" on page 63).

```
library(widyr)

newsgroup_cors <- words_by_newsgroup %>%
  pairwise_cor(newsgroup, word, n, sort = TRUE)

newsgroup_cors
```

```
## # A tibble: 380 × 3
##                         item1                     item2 correlation
##                         <chr>                     <chr>       <dbl>
## 1         talk.religion.misc     soc.religion.christian   0.8347275
## 2     soc.religion.christian         talk.religion.misc   0.8347275
## 3               alt.atheism         talk.religion.misc   0.7793079
## 4         talk.religion.misc               alt.atheism   0.7793079
## 5               alt.atheism     soc.religion.christian   0.7510723
## 6     soc.religion.christian               alt.atheism   0.7510723
## 7       comp.sys.mac.hardware    comp.sys.ibm.pc.hardware   0.6799043
## 8    comp.sys.ibm.pc.hardware      comp.sys.mac.hardware   0.6799043
## 9           rec.sport.baseball         rec.sport.hockey   0.5770378
## 10            rec.sport.hockey       rec.sport.baseball   0.5770378
## # ... with 370 more rows
```

We could then filter for stronger correlations among newsgroups and visualize them in a network (Figure 9-3).

```
library(ggraph)
library(igraph)
set.seed(2017)

newsgroup_cors %>%
  filter(correlation > .4) %>%
  graph_from_data_frame() %>%
  ggraph(layout = "fr") +
  geom_edge_link(aes(alpha = correlation, width = correlation)) +
  geom_node_point(size = 6, color = "lightblue") +
  geom_node_text(aes(label = name), repel = TRUE) +
  theme_void()
```

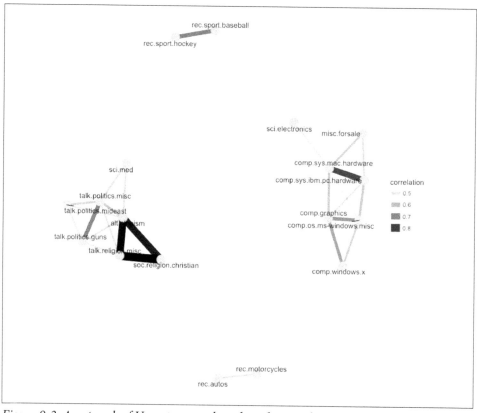

Figure 9-3. A network of Usenet groups based on the correlation of word counts between them, including only connections with a correlation greater than 0.4

It looks like there are four main clusters of newsgroups: computers/electronics, politics/religion, motor vehicles, and sports. This certainly makes sense in terms of what words and topics we'd expect these newsgroups to have in common.

Topic Modeling

In Chapter 6, we used the latent Dirichlet allocation (LDA) algorithm to divide a set of chapters into the books they originally came from. Could LDA do the same to sort out Usenet messages that come from different newsgroups?

Let's try dividing up messages from the four science-related newsgroups. We first process these into a document-term matrix with `cast_dtm()` ("Casting Tidy Text Data into a Matrix" on page 77), then fit the model with the `LDA()` function from the topicmodels package.

```
# include only words that occur at least 50 times
word_sci_newsgroups <- usenet_words %>%
```

```
  filter(str_detect(newsgroup, "^sci")) %>%
  group_by(word) %>%
  mutate(word_total = n()) %>%
  ungroup() %>%
  filter(word_total > 50)

# convert into a document-term matrix
# with document names such as sci.crypt_14147
sci_dtm <- word_sci_newsgroups %>%
  unite(document, newsgroup, id) %>%
  count(document, word) %>%
  cast_dtm(document, word, n)

library(topicmodels)
sci_lda <- LDA(sci_dtm, k = 4, control = list(seed = 2016))
```

What four topics did this model extract, and do they match the four newsgroups? This approach will look familiar from Chapter 6: we visualize each topic based on the most frequent terms within it (Figure 9-4).

```
sci_lda %>%
  tidy() %>%
  group_by(topic) %>%
  top_n(8, beta) %>%
  ungroup() %>%
  mutate(term = reorder(term, beta)) %>%
  ggplot(aes(term, beta, fill = factor(topic))) +
  geom_col(show.legend = FALSE) +
  facet_wrap(~ topic, scales = "free_y") +
  coord_flip()
```

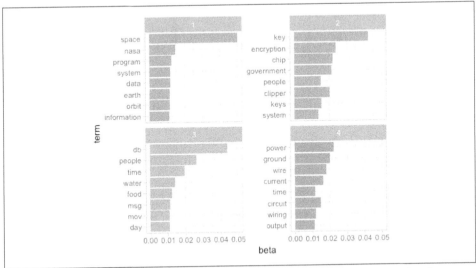

Figure 9-4. The top eight words from each topic fit by LDA on the science-related news-groups

From the top words, we can start to suspect which topics may capture which newsgroups. Topic 1 certainly represents the sci.space newsgroup (thus the most common word being "space"), and topic 2 is likely drawn from cryptography, with terms such as "key" and "encryption." Just as we did in "Document-Topic Probabilities" on page 95, we can confirm this by seeing how documents from each newsgroup have higher "gamma" for each topic (Figure 9-5).

```
sci_lda %>%
  tidy(matrix = "gamma") %>%
  separate(document, c("newsgroup", "id"), sep = "_") %>%
  mutate(newsgroup = reorder(newsgroup, gamma * topic)) %>%
  ggplot(aes(factor(topic), gamma)) +
  geom_boxplot() +
  facet_wrap(~ newsgroup) +
  labs(x = "Topic",
       y = "# of messages where this was the highest % topic")
```

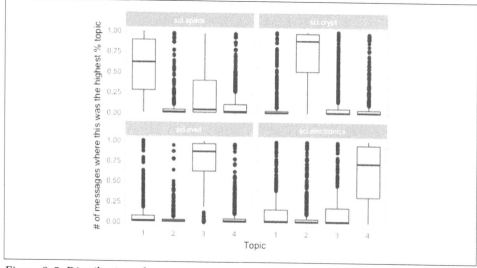

Figure 9-5. Distribution of gamma for each topic within each Usenet newsgroup

Much as we saw in the literature analysis, topic modeling was able to discover the distinct topics present in the text without needing to consult the labels.

Notice that the division of Usenet messages isn't as clean as the division of book chapters, with a substantial number of messages from each newsgroup getting high values of "gamma" for other topics. This isn't surprising since many of the messages are short and could overlap in terms of common words (for example, discussions of space travel could include many of the same words as discussions of electronics). This is a realistic example of how LDA might divide documents into rough topics while still allowing a degree of overlap.

Sentiment Analysis

We can use the sentiment analysis techniques we explored in Chapter 2 to examine how often positive and negative words occur in these Usenet posts. Which newsgroups are the most positive or negative overall?

In this example we'll use the AFINN sentiment lexicon, which provides numeric positivity scores for each word, and visualize it with a bar plot (Figure 9-6).

```
newsgroup_sentiments <- words_by_newsgroup %>%
  inner_join(get_sentiments("afinn"), by = "word") %>%
  group_by(newsgroup) %>%
  summarize(score = sum(score * n) / sum(n))

newsgroup_sentiments %>%
  mutate(newsgroup = reorder(newsgroup, score)) %>%
  ggplot(aes(newsgroup, score, fill = score > 0)) +
  geom_col(show.legend = FALSE) +
  coord_flip() +
  ylab("Average sentiment score")
```

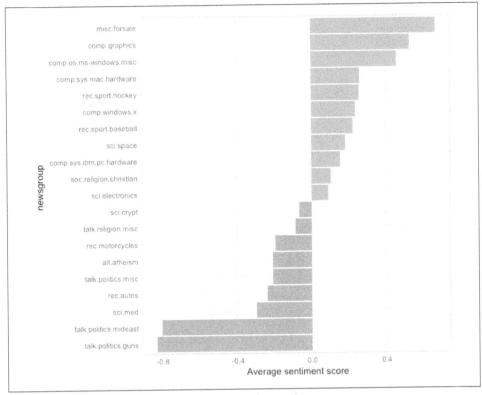

Figure 9-6. Average AFINN score for posts within each newsgroup

According to this analysis, the misc.forsale newsgroup is the most positive. This makes sense, since it likely includes many positive adjectives about the products that users want to sell!

Sentiment Analysis by Word

It's worth looking deeper to understand *why* some newsgroups end up more positive or negative than others. For that, we can examine the total positive and negative contributions of each word.

```
contributions <- usenet_words %>%
  inner_join(get_sentiments("afinn"), by = "word") %>%
  group_by(word) %>%
  summarize(occurences = n(),
            contribution = sum(score))

contributions

## # A tibble: 1,909 × 3
##           word occurences contribution
##          <chr>      <int>        <int>
## 1      abandon         13          -26
## 2    abandoned         19          -38
## 3     abandons          3           -6
## 4    abduction          2           -4
## 5        abhor          4          -12
## 6     abhorred          1           -3
## 7    abhorrent          2           -6
## 8    abilities         16           32
## 9      ability        177          354
## 10      aboard          8            8
## # ... with 1,899 more rows
```

Which words have the most effect on sentiment scores overall (Figure 9-7)?

```
contributions %>%
  top_n(25, abscontribution) %>%
  mutate(word = reorder(word, contribution)) %>%
  ggplot(aes(word, contribution, fill = contribution > 0)) +
  geom_col(show.legend = FALSE) +
  coord_flip()
```

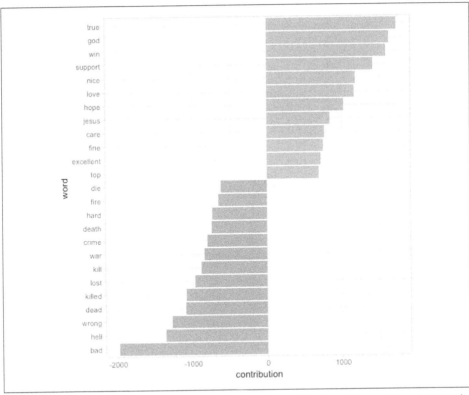

Figure 9-7. Words with the greatest contributions to positive/negative sentiment scores in the Usenet text

These words look generally reasonable as indicators of each message's sentiment, but we can spot possible problems with the approach. "True" could just as easily be a part of "not true" or a similar negative expression, and the words "God" and "Jesus" are apparently very common on Usenet but could easily be used in many contexts, positive or negative.

We may also care about which words contribute the most *within each newsgroup*, so that we can see which newsgroups might be incorrectly estimated. We can calculate each word's contribution to each newsgroup's sentiment score, and visualize the strongest contributors from a selection of the groups (Figure 9-8).

```
top_sentiment_words <- words_by_newsgroup %>%
  inner_join(get_sentiments("afinn"), by = "word") %>%
  mutate(contribution = score * n / sum(n))

top_sentiment_words

## # A tibble: 13,063 × 5
##                newsgroup   word      n score contribution
```

```
##                              <chr> <chr> <int> <int>        <dbl>
## 1  soc.religion.christian       god   917     1  0.014418012
## 2  soc.religion.christian     jesus   440     1  0.006918130
## 3       talk.politics.guns       gun   425    -1 -0.006682285
## 4       talk.religion.misc       god   296     1  0.004654015
## 5            alt.atheism        god   268     1  0.004213770
## 6  soc.religion.christian     faith   257     1  0.004040817
## 7       talk.religion.misc     jesus   256     1  0.004025094
## 8     talk.politics.mideast   killed   202    -3 -0.009528152
## 9     talk.politics.mideast      war   187    -2 -0.005880411
## 10 soc.religion.christian      true   179     2  0.005628842
## # ... with 13,053 more rows
```

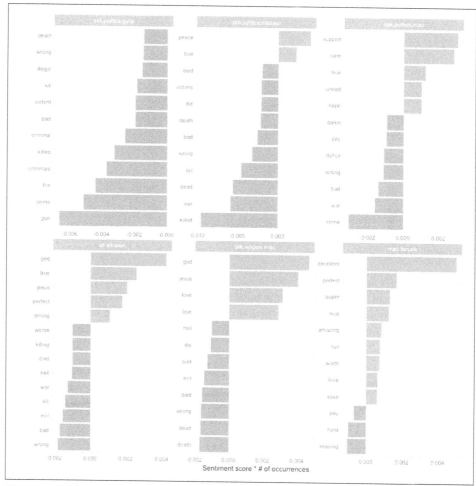

Figure 9-8. The 12 words that contributed the most to sentiment scores within each of 6 newsgroups

This confirms our hypothesis about the misc.forsale newsgroup: most of the sentiment is driven by positive adjectives such as "excellent" and "perfect." We can also see how much sentiment is confounded with topic. An atheism newsgroup is likely to discuss "god" in detail even in a negative context, and we can see that it makes the newsgroup look more positive. Similarly, the negative contribution of the word "gun" to the talk.politics.guns group will occur even when the members are discussing guns positively.

This helps remind us that sentiment analysis can be confounded by topic, and that we should always examine the influential words before interpreting the analysis too deeply.

Sentiment Analysis by Message

We can also try finding the most positive and negative individual messages by grouping and summarizing by id rather than newsgroup.

```
sentiment_messages <- usenet_words %>%
  inner_join(get_sentiments("afinn"), by = "word") %>%
  group_by(newsgroup, id) %>%
  summarize(sentiment = mean(score),
            words = n()) %>%
  ungroup() %>%
  filter(words >= 5)
```

As a simple measure to reduce the role of randomness, we filtered out messages that had fewer than five words that contributed to sentiment.

What were the most positive messages?

```
sentiment_messages %>%
  arrange(desc(sentiment))
```

```
## # A tibble: 3,554 × 4
##                   newsgroup     id sentiment words
##                       <chr>  <chr>     <dbl> <int>
## 1          rec.sport.hockey  53560  3.888889    18
## 2          rec.sport.hockey  53602  3.833333    30
## 3          rec.sport.hockey  53822  3.833333     6
## 4          rec.sport.hockey  53645  3.230769    13
## 5                 rec.autos 102768  3.200000     5
## 6               misc.forsale  75965  3.000000     5
## 7               misc.forsale  76037  3.000000     5
## 8        rec.sport.baseball 104458  3.000000    11
## 9          rec.sport.hockey  53571  3.000000     5
## 10  comp.os.ms-windows.misc   9620  2.857143     7
## # ... with 3,544 more rows
```

Let's check this by looking at the most positive message in the whole dataset. To assist in this, we could write a short function for printing a specified message.

```
print_message <- function(group, message_id) {
  result <- cleaned_text %>%
    filter(newsgroup == group, id == message_id, text != "")

  cat(result$text, sep = "\n")
}

print_message("rec.sport.hockey", 53560)

## Everybody.  Please send me your predictions for the Stanley Cup Playoffs!
## I want to see who people think will win.!!!!!!!
## Please Send them in this format, or something comparable:
## 1. Winner of Buffalo-Boston
## 2. Winner of Montreal-Quebec
## 3. Winner of Pittsburgh-New York
## 4. Winner of New Jersey-Washington
## 5. Winner of Chicago-(Minnesota/St.Louis)
## 6. Winner of Toronto-Detroit
## 7. Winner of Vancouver-Winnipeg
## 8. Winner of Calgary-Los Angeles
## 9. Winner of Adams Division (1-2 above)
## 10. Winner of Patrick Division (3-4 above)
## 11. Winner of Norris Division (5-6 above)
## 12. Winner of Smythe Division (7-8 above)
## 13. Winner of Wales Conference (9-10 above)
## 14. Winner of Campbell Conference (11-12 above)
## 15. Winner of Stanley Cup (13-14 above)
## I will summarize the predictions, and see who is the biggest
## INTERNET GURU PREDICTING GUY/GAL.
## Send entries to Richard Madison
## rrmadiso@napier.uwaterloo.ca
## PS:  I will send my entries to one of you folks so you know when I say
## I won, that I won!!!!!
```

It looks like this message was chosen because it uses the word "winner" many times. How about the most negative message? Turns out it's also from the hockey site, but has a very different attitude.

```
sentiment_messages %>%
  arrange(sentiment)

## # A tibble: 3,554 × 4
##                newsgroup      id sentiment words
##                    <chr>   <chr>     <dbl> <int>
## 1      rec.sport.hockey   53907 -3.000000     6
## 2        sci.electronics   53899 -3.000000     5
## 3   talk.politics.mideast  75918 -3.000000     7
## 4              rec.autos  101627 -2.833333     6
## 5          comp.graphics   37948 -2.800000     5
## 6          comp.windows.x  67204 -2.700000    10
```

```
## 7        talk.politics.guns  53362 -2.666667       6
## 8               alt.atheism  51309 -2.600000       5
## 9   comp.sys.mac.hardware  51513 -2.600000       5
## 10                rec.autos 102883 -2.600000       5
## # ... with 3,544 more rows
```

```
print_message("rec.sport.hockey", 53907)
```

```
## Losers like us? You are the fucking moron who has never heard of the Western
## Business School, or the University of Western Ontario for that matter. Why
## don't you pull your head out of your asshole and smell something other than
## shit for once so you can look on a map to see where UWO is! Back to hockey,
## the North Stars should be moved because for the past few years they have
## just been SHIT. A real team like Toronto would never be moved!!!
## Andrew--
```

Well, we can confidently say that the sentiment analysis worked!

N-gram Analysis

In Chapter 4, we considered the effect of words such as "not" and "no" on sentiment analysis of Jane Austen novels, such as considering whether a phrase like "don't like" led to passages incorrectly being labeled as positive. The Usenet dataset is a much larger corpus of more modern text, so we may be interested in how sentiment analysis may be reversed in this text.

We'll start by finding and counting all the bigrams in the Usenet posts.

```
usenet_bigrams <- cleaned_text %>%
  unnest_tokens(bigram, text, token = "ngrams", n = 2)

usenet_bigram_counts <- usenet_bigrams %>%
  count(newsgroup, bigram, sort = TRUE) %>%
  ungroup() %>%
  separate(bigram, c("word1", "word2"), sep = " ")
```

We could then define a list of six words that we suspect are used in negation, such as "no," "not," and "without," and visualize the sentiment-associated words that most often follow them (Figure 9-9). This shows the words that most often contribute in the "wrong" direction.

```
negate_words <- c("not", "without", "no", "can't", "don't", "won't")

usenet_bigram_counts %>%
  filter(word1 %in% negate_words) %>%
  count(word1, word2, wt = n, sort = TRUE) %>%
  inner_join(get_sentiments("afinn"), by = c(word2 = "word")) %>%
  mutate(contribution = score * nn) %>%
  group_by(word1) %>%
  top_n(10, abs(contribution)) %>%
  ungroup() %>%
  mutate(word2 = reorder(paste(word2, word1, sep = "__"), contribution)) %>%
  ggplot(aes(word2, contribution, fill = contribution > 0)) +
```

```
geom_col(show.legend = FALSE) +
facet_wrap(~ word1, scales = "free", nrow = 3) +
scale_x_discrete(labels = function(x) gsub("__.+$", "", x)) +
xlab("Words preceded by a negation") +
ylab("Sentiment score * # of occurrences") +
theme(axis.text.x = element_text(angle = 90, hjust = 1)) +
coord_flip()
```

Figure 9-9. Words that contribute the most to sentiment when they follow a "negating" word

It looks like the largest sources of misidentifying a word as positive come from "don't want/like/care," and the largest source of incorrectly classified negative sentiment is "no problem."

Summary

In this analysis of Usenet messages, we've incorporated almost every method for tidy text mining described in this book, ranging from tf-idf to topic modeling, and from sentiment analysis to n-gram tokenization. Throughout the chapter, and indeed through all of our case studies, we've been able to rely on a small list of common tools for exploration and visualization. We hope that these examples show how much all tidy text analyses have in common with each other, and indeed with all tidy data analyses.

Bibliography

Abelson, Hal. 2008. "Foreword." In *Essentials of Programming Languages, 3rd Edition*. The MIT Press.

Arnold, Taylor B. 2016. "cleanNLP: A Tidy Data Model for Natural Language Processing." *https://cran.r-project.org/package=cleanNLP*.

Arnold, Taylor, and Lauren Tilton. 2016. "coreNLP: Wrappers Around Stanford Corenlp Tools." *https://cran.r-project.org/package=coreNLP*.

Benoit, Kenneth, and Paul Nulty. 2016. "quanteda: Quantitative Analysis of Textual Data." *https://CRAN.R-project.org/package=quanteda*.

Feinerer, Ingo, Kurt Hornik, and David Meyer. 2008. "Text Mining Infrastructure in R." *Journal of Statistical Software* 25 (5): 1–54. *http://www.jstatsoft.org/v25/i05/*.

Loughran, Tim, and Bill McDonald. 2011. "When Is a Liability Not a Liability? Textual Analysis, Dictionaries, and 10-Ks." *The Journal of Finance* 66 (1): 35–65. doi: *https://doi.org/10.1111/j.1540-6261.2010.01625.x*.

Mimno, David. 2013. "mallet: A Wrapper Around the Java Machine Learning Tool Mallet." *https://cran.r-project.org/package=mallet*.

Mullen, Lincoln. 2016. "tokenizers: A Consistent Interface to Tokenize Natural Language Text." *https://cran.r-project.org/package=tokenizers*.

Pedersen, Thomas Lin. 2017. "ggraph: An Implementation of Grammar of Graphics for Graphs and Networks." *https://cran.r-project.org/package=ggraph*.

Rinker, Tyler W. 2017. "sentimentr: Calculate Text Polarity Sentiment." Buffalo, New York: University at Buffalo/SUNY. *http://github.com/trinker/sentimentr*.

Robinson, David. 2016. "gutenbergr: Download and Process Public Domain Works from Project Gutenberg." *https://cran.rstudio.com/package=gutenbergr*.

———. 2017. "broom: Convert Statistical Analysis Objects into Tidy Data Frames." *https://cran.r-project.org/package=broom*.

Silge, Julia. 2016. "janeaustenr: Jane Austen's Complete Novels." *https://cran.r-project.org/package=janeaustenr*.

Silge, Julia, and David Robinson. 2016. "tidytext: Text Mining and Analysis Using Tidy Data Principles in R." *The Journal of Open Source Software* 1 (3). doi: *https://doi.org/10.21105/joss.00037*.

Wickham, Hadley. 2007. "Reshaping Data with the reshape Package." *Journal of Statistical Software* 21 (12): 1–20. *http://www.jstatsoft.org/v21/i12/*.

———. 2009. *ggplot2: Elegant Graphics for Data Analysis*. Springer-Verlag New York. *http://ggplot2.org*.

———. 2014. "Tidy Data." *Journal of Statistical Software* 59 (1): 1–23. doi: 10.18637/jss.v059.i10 (*https://doi.org/10.18637/jss.v059.i10*).

———. 2016. "tidyr: Easily Tidy Data with 'spread()' and 'gather()' Functions." *https://cran.r-project.org/package=tidyr*.

Wickham, Hadley, and Romain Francois. 2016. "dplyr: A Grammar of Data Manipulation." *https://cran.r-project.org/package=dplyr*.

Index

N

n-grams, 45-61
  (see also bigrams)
  counting and filtering, 46-48
  tokenizing by, 45-61
  Usenet text analysis, 169-171
NASA metadata mining (case study), 125-152
  calculating tf-idf for description fields, 137-140
  casting to DocumentTermMatrix, 140
  connecting description fields to keywords, 138-140
  connecting topic modeling with keywords, 149-152
  data organization at NASA, 126-130
  data wrangling/tidying, 126-128
  interpreting the topic model, 142-149
  networks of description/title words, 131-133
  networks of keywords, 134-137
  simple exploration of common words, 129
  topic modeling, 140-152
  word co-occurrences/correlations, 130-137
negation, terms of, 51-54, 169-171
networks
  description/title words, 131-133
  of keywords, 134-137
  visualizing with ggraph, 54-58
nontidy formats, converting to/from tidy text format, 69-87
NRC lexicon
  characteristics of, 14
  Pride and Prejudice sentiment calculations, 22

O

one-token-per-row framework, 1
opinion mining, 13
  (see also sentiment analysis)

P

pairwise correlation, 63-67
Pearson correlation, 64
per-document-per-topic probabilities (gamma), 95, 100-103
per-topic-per-word probabilities (beta), 91-95, 103-107
phi coefficient, 63
physics texts, tf-idf for corpus of, 40-44

preprocessing, 155
presidential inauguration speeches, dfm objects and, 74-77
Pride and Prejudice (Austen)
  as test case for comparing sentiment lexicons, 19-22
  common bigrams in, 57-58
  correlations among sections, 62, 66-67
Project Gutenberg, 7, 40

Q

qualifiers, 16
quanteda package, 74-77

R

rank, Zipf's law and, 34
regex patterns, 27, 111
relationships between words (see correlations)
  (see n-grams)

S

sentiment analysis, 13-29
  bigrams for context in, 51-54
  by message, 167-169
  by word, 164-167
  comparing three sentiment lexicons, 19-22
  lexicons in sentiments dataset, 14-16, 84-87
  most common positive/negative words, 22-24
  sentiments dataset, 14-16
  text analysis flowchart, 13
  units larger than a single word, 27-29
  Usenet case study, 163-171
  with inner join, 16-19
  with tidy data, 13-29
  wordclouds, 25
sentiment lexicons, 14-16
  (see also specific lexicons)
  Pride and Prejudice as test case for comparing, 19-22
separate(), 47
sparse matrices, 70, 78
stop words
  bigrams as, 47
  defined, 6
  removing from NASA data, 128, 130
string, text stored as, 2

About the Authors

Julia Silge is a data scientist at Stack Overflow; her work involves analyzing complex datasets and communicating about technical topics with diverse audiences. She has a PhD in astrophysics and loves Jane Austen and making beautiful charts. Julia worked in academia and ed tech before moving into data science and discovering the statistical programming language R.

David Robinson is a data scientist at Stack Overflow with a PhD in Quantitative and Computational Biology from Princeton University. He enjoys developing open source R packages, including broom, gganimate, fuzzyjoin, and widyr, as well as blogging about statistics, R, and text mining on his blog, Variance Explained (*http://varianceex plained.org/*).

Colophon

The animal on the cover of *Text Mining with R* is the European rabbit (*Oryctolagus cuniculus*), a small mammal native to Spain, Portugal, and North Africa. They are now found throughout the world, having been introduced by European settlers. Due to a lack of natural predators, they are classified as an invasive species in some regions.

European rabbits are generally grey-brown in color and range from 34 to 50 centimeters in length. They have powerful hind legs with heavily padded feet that allow them to quickly hop from place to place. As social animals, European rabbits live together in small groups known as warrens. They eat grass, seeds, bark, roots, and vegetables.

European rabbits have been domesticated for several centuries, going back to the Roman Empire. Raising rabbits for their meat, wool, or fur is known as cuniculture. They are also commonly kept as pets. Over time, several different breeds have been developed, such as the Angora or the Holland Lop.

Many of the animals on O'Reilly covers are endangered; all of them are important to the world. To learn more about how you can help, go to *animals.oreilly.com*.

The cover image is from *History of British Quadrupeds*. The cover fonts are URW Typewriter and Guardian Sans. The text font is Adobe Minion Pro; the heading font is Adobe Myriad Condensed; and the code font is Dalton Maag's Ubuntu Mono.

Learn from experts.
Find the answers you need.

Sign up for a **10-day free trial** to get **unlimited access** to all of the content on Safari, including Learning Paths, interactive tutorials, and curated playlists that draw from thousands of ebooks and training videos on a wide range of topics, including data, design, DevOps, management, business—and much more.

Start your free trial at:

oreilly.com/safari

(No credit card required.)

Milton Keynes UK
Ingram Content Group UK Ltd.
UKHW010942300724
446286UK00002B/2